IMAGES
of Sport

SALFORD
RUGBY LEAGUE CLUB

The all-action attacking style of Paul Charlton. The gritty Cumbrian, who was signed from Workington Town for £12,500 in October 1969, is rated by many as Salford's finest full-back.

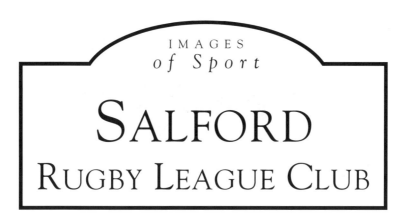

IMAGES
of Sport

SALFORD
RUGBY LEAGUE CLUB

Compiled by
Graham Morris

TEMPUS

First published 2000
Copyright © Graham Morris, 2000

Tempus Publishing Limited
The Mill, Brimscombe Port,
Stroud, Gloucestershire, GL5 2QG

ISBN 0 7524 1897 1

Typesetting and origination by
Tempus Publishing Limited
Printed in Great Britain by
Midway Clark Printing, Wiltshire

Front cover: Gus Risman, the victorious Salford captain, is hoisted shoulder high by his colleagues as they parade around the Wembley pitch. The Red Devils had just achieved their greatest triumph in defeating Barrow to win the Rugby League Challenge Cup of 1938.

Also Available from Tempus

Bradford Bulls RLFC	Robert Gate	0 7524 1896 3
Castleford RLFC	David Smart	0 7524 1895 5
Halifax RLFC	Andrew Hardcastle	0 7524 1831 9
Headingley RLFC Voices	Phil Caplan	0 7524 1822 X
Hunslet RLFC	Les Hoole	0 7524 1641 3
Leeds RLFC	Phil Caplan & Les Hoole	0 7524 1140 3
Sheffield Eagles RLFC	John Cornwell	0 7524 1830 0
St Helens RLFC	Alex Service	0 7524 1883 1
Warrington RLFC	Gary Slater & Eddie Fuller	0 7524 1870 X
Yorkshire Rugby League	Les Hoole	0 7524 1881 5
The Five Nations Story	David Hands	0 7524 1851 3

(All books are 128 page softbacks with the exception of *The Five Nations Story* which is a 176 page hardback with colour illustrations.)

Contents

Acknowledgements

It would be impossible to compile a book such as this without the help of others. The majority of the material contained in these pages has been taken from my own collection, built up over a lifetime of following my childhood heroes. The rest, particularly that covering the past decade, has recently been added specifically for this publication. In both cases I am indebted to the many people who, like myself, share a love and passion for the game of Rugby League. Some of those acknowledged here may have forgotten the help they gave me, often years ago, and others, sadly, are no longer with us. Hopefully, I have not overlooked anyone. Where necessary, I have made all reasonable effort to trace copyright holders for permission to use their pictures. My appreciation then to: Timothy Auty, Trevor Delaney, Robert Gate, Albert Gear, Andrew Hardcastle, Percy Harrison, Bert Hughes, John Jenkins, Hilda Johnson, Michael Latham, Charlie Neill, Ron Robinson, Brian Rosson, Irvin Saxton, Brian Snape, Tom Webb and Graham Williams. I am also thankful to the following organisations for generously allowing me the use of their photographs: the *Manchester Evening News* (particularly sports editor Pete Spencer, Chris Brierley and Dave Thomas), the *Advertiser & Salford City Reporter* (Jonathan Greaney and Bill McLaughlin) and the *Rugby Leaguer* (Gerald Webster and Vivian Haydock). My gratitude also extends to the staff of the Salford Local History Library who, as always, provided invaluable help. Finally, but not least, my special thanks to David Tarry, the chief executive of the Salford Rugby League Club, not only for his help, but also his endorsement of this publication on behalf of the club.

Emlyn Jenkins (left) and Billy Watkins formed one of the most exciting half-back combinations ever seen at Salford. The two Welsh stars were first paired together in a Salford jersey in September 1931 and went on to partner each other 183 times until Jenkins transferred to Wigan in 1938. They were also a first choice at international level and represented Great Britain in the tour to Australia and New Zealand in 1936.

Introduction

Over 100 years ago, the members of the Salford Football Club voted to resign from the English Rugby Football Union. This historic decision was taken at the climax of an emotional and highly charged meeting that took place at the Hope Board School, situated in Liverpool Street, Salford, on 16 April 1896. The defectors elected to join the infant Northern Union, known today as the Rugby Football League, founded just eight months earlier by twenty of the North's senior rugby clubs.

The Northern Union had finally seen the light of day after several years of dispute between the clubs and the English RFU over many issues, the most publicised and controversial being the payment of 'broken-time' to players. This was, in effect, compensation paid to the (essentially) working class men for the loss of Saturday wages to turn out for their clubs. At the time, it was viewed as either a brave or a foolhardy decision by Salford, such was the deep and bitter divide amongst sports enthusiasts as to the merits of joining the rebels.

It is difficult to say with any confidence as to what the status of the Salford Rugby Football Club would be today had it remained in membership of the RFU. Indeed, would it still exist given that most of the major clubs in the region had already severed connections? What can be stated with certainty, whatever the pros and cons, is that Salford has survived for almost 130 years and is now an established and famous name in the modern sports loving world and the game of Rugby League in particular.

Over the past century, generations of devoted Salford supporters have turned up eagerly at The Willows, the club's home since 1901, and been fortunate enough to cheer for some of the most legendary names seen in the sport. Famous players like Jimmy Lomas, Willie Thomas, Gus Risman, Barney Hudson, Chris Hesketh and David Watkins spring immediately to mind, but in truth the list is virtually endless. Whilst they have thrilled the Salford public on the pitch, great administrators have also played a vital and, often unsung, part off it. Lance Todd, Brian Snape and John Wilkinson are just a few of the many. Hopefully, I will do justice to all of them in the pages that follow.

One of the most compelling messages I felt in compiling the material for this book are the number of, sadly, forgotten names of the past to whom so much is owed. Most of us are aware of the contribution of those mentioned above, but how many will realise the debt that is owed to pioneering committeemen like James Higson and Archie Sutherland? What do we know about some of the club's early star performers? Who could name the four Salford players included in the first ever rugby tour to the Antipodes in 1888? How could those hardy souls even contemplate representing club and country on a journey lasting eight months, that covered the length and breadth of Australia and New Zealand, before the day of the jet plane and luxury coach? Those tourists played 52 matches and Salford's Harry Eagles appeared in every single one of them! These are the people that laid the solid foundation from which the Salford Rugby League Club has been built.

It is also clear that much of what has been achieved by the men in the famous red jersey is due, in no small way, to the strong Welsh connection that the club has enjoyed over the years. Many of the major individual record holders are from the principality and, indeed, some of the most celebrated captains in the history of the club originally came north from the valleys. In fact, barely a trophy of note has been won down the years without a few Welshmen around and, when Salford finally brought the Rugby League Challenge Cup home from Wembley in 1938, there were no fewer than eight in the team.

Compiling the material for this book has been a labour of love containing, as it does, the most comprehensive set of photographs and illustrations of the Salford Rugby League Club ever assembled into one volume. As the *Images of Sport* title implies, this is a story told in pictures as well as in words. It is not intended to be a comprehensive history, but the reader will, nonetheless, be taken on a journey through the life and times of this great club. We travel from humble beginnings at the Cavendish Street school in Hulme in 1873, through the peaks of joy and troughs of despair, to arrive at the present day and the high profile status enjoyed by the renamed Salford City Reds. In doing so, I have tried to recapture the spirit of those early pioneers of the nineteenth century, relive the traumatic moments since and to reflect on the glory associated with the Lance Todd and Brian Snape dynasties. All the great names, some might say 'legends', of the Salford Rugby League Club are covered, including many of the hard working administrators of the past, who often succeeded against adversity to take the club a stage further along the path to greatness.

This volume has been broken down into seven chronological chapters, each covering a specific period in the evolution of the club. You could, however, claim that the last chapter of this book is incomplete! I have given it the title of 'The Wilkinson Years' covering, as it does, John Wilkinson's long reign as chairman from 1982. I believe that, more than any chairman previously associated with the club, he has had to endure some of the sport's most difficult and trying times. The challenges have been many and varied: the Safety of Sports Grounds Act, the advent of full-time professionalism, threatened mergers and the adjustment to a summer schedule are all examples of what has had to be faced and then addressed. That he has succeeded in meeting those challenges can be judged by the healthy state of the Salford Rugby League club today.

Finally, whether young or not so young, I hope and trust that you will both meet and rediscover your own particular favourites in these pages or perhaps be introduced to a few new heroes from the club's rich heritage. If you take as much pleasure from reading this as I had in assembling the material then I will have done my job well.

Graham Morris
Worsley, June 2000

Six Salford players display their Lancashire county jerseys in 1903. From left to right, back row: George Heath, Pat Tunney, George Cooke (trainer). Front row: Jack Rhapps, Dan Smith, Jimmy Lomas, Herbert Buckler. Tunney's 18 Lancashire caps is the most achieved by a Salford player during the club's post-Rugby Union period.

One

From Cavendish Street to Salford

1873-1895

The earliest known team photograph of the Salford club is this studio study taken during the 1887/88 season. Although there are no surviving captions associated with this line-up, we can identify captain Sam Williams (front row, centre), Harry Eagles (middle row in white England jersey) and future England cap Tom Kent (middle row, extreme right). Formed by the boys of the Cavendish Street Chapel in Hulme, Manchester, in 1873, the team had begun life playing on an adjoining field before moving to a pitch at Moss Vale in Moss Side. By 1875, they had crossed the River Irwell into Salford and have remained in Salford ever since. Through the 1880s the club had grown in stature following the amalgamation with the Crescent Football Club in 1881. In 1886, Salford went through 21 matches unbeaten and then, in 1887, had a run of 22 matches without defeat.

Peel Park was the site of the first home for the Crescent Football Club when they began as a schoolboy side in 1876. In 1880, they transferred to the Mile Field, off Trafford Road. It was when Salford amalgamated with the Crescent that the club really took off in the public consciousness. Many of Salford's most famous players of the time began their careers in the Crescent ranks. Peel Park was also the original base for Broughton Rangers, a famous Rugby League side who, sadly, disbanded in 1955. The park, shown in this picture, was featured in David Lean's classic 1952 film *Love on the Dole*, which starred Charles Laughton and (Sir) John Mills.

Salford used the Clowes Hotel on Trafford Road as their headquarters from 1877 until 1889. The players also had changing facilities there. It was at the Clowes Hotel in 1881 that several key meetings which shaped the future of the club were held. The Salford team was struggling on the field and lacked credibility with the locals because they had few Salford-born players. William Allen, who became Salford's honorary secretary during the period, wanted the club to merge with two local junior sides, Stanley, from the Seedley district of Salford, and the Crescent. An initial meeting proved unsuccessful, but a second was arranged at the Clowes with representatives of the Crescent. James Higson, secretary of the Crescent club and destined for the same role at Salford, was equally enthusiastic about the merger and agreement was reached. This was a turning point for Salford. Only 26 matches, out of 263 played, were lost during the remainder of that decade and interest in the club increased rapidly.

Without doubt, the most celebrated player in Salford's early history was Harry Eagles, captured by this illustration for the sports publication *Black and White* in October 1887. Although only 5ft 6½ins tall, Eagles was well known for his industrious play and was considered a proverbial tower of strength in the pack where he would lead the way with shouts of 'follow me!'. A former Crescent player, he played 265 times for Salford between 1881 and 1893, scoring 63 tries, placing him third in both appearance and try-scoring charts for the club during the Rugby Union period to 1896. He captained the team in 1888/89 and 1890/91 and was the first player from Salford to receive international selection in 1888. Unfortunately, England's dispute with the other home unions meant he never played, although he still received his international cap and jersey. He appeared in all 52 matches of Great Britain's first tour of Australia and New Zealand in 1888, a record unequalled in Rugby Union since. He represented Lancashire 18 times during the 1886-90 period, and played in three of the annual North versus South clashes between 1887 and 1890. Away from rugby, his bravery was recognised by the award of the Salford Hundred Humane Society Medal for rescuing four people from drowning.

Sam Williams made 170 appearances for Salford between the years 1881 and 1890, being captain in seasons 1887/88 and 1889/90. Along with Harry Eagles, Tom Kent and Jack Anderton, he represented the club in the first ever Rugby Union tour to Australia and New Zealand in 1888, playing in 50 of the 52 tour matches, a figure bettered only by Eagles. He was a forward who was noted for his high work rate and leadership qualities and, like so many of his colleagues, he began his rugby career with the Crescent. In 1886/87 he was capped four times for Lancashire and, in the same season, became the first Salford player to be selected for the prestigious North versus South representative match, played at Blackheath on that occasion.

William Buckley was yet another of the talented players that Salford acquired in their merger with the Crescent club. He played in 87 games for Salford between 1881 and 1885 and was the club captain during the period 1883 to 1885. Although a forward, he was known for his pace and was reportedly adept at the long forgotten forwards' art of dribbling with the ball.

The 'Father' of the Salford Rugby Club is considered to be Archie A. Sutherland. In 1879, when he was the honorary secretary of the club, he agitated for a name change from Cavendish to Salford which, he believed, would have wider appeal and bring about an improved fixture list. Despite opposition from the other members, he finally got his way and his foresight and initiative almost certainly ensured the future of the club. He had played regularly for Cavendish from 1874, mostly as a centre three-quarter. After the change of name to Salford he played just 30 more matches before, surprisingly, joining Swinton in 1882. As well as being an administrator, Sutherland was a noted sports journalist.

Hugh Williamson was the first captain of Salford following the merger with Crescent and he continued to lead he side until 1883, when injury all but forced his retirement. He managed to play spasmodically until 1886 before finally calling it a day. Starting as a forward and then transferring to the wing, he scored 24 tries in just 50 matches. He also represented Cheshire.

Salford long believed they were being overlooked by the county committee when it came to picking the side to represent Lancashire and made many representations to the selectors. The feeling was that the club's success was not being reflected properly. One journalist, in 1885, wrote about 'the unfair prejudice existing against the club'. That finally changed when twenty-seven-year-old James Jackson played against Durham on 30 January 1886, after initially being picked to face Yorkshire at Huddersfield earlier in season, but withdrawing due to illness. Due to the prestige associated with county selection, it led to greater recognition for the club – resulting in improved fixtures and a seat on the county committee. Looking back, it can be viewed as the first major honour for Salford. Following Jackson's breakthrough, eight Salford players would make county debuts in the next three seasons for Lancashire. This drawing of Jackson appeared in the *Cricketer's Herald and Football Times* in December 1885.

MR. JACKSON, of the Salford Team.

1884.	CLUB.	GROUND.	RESULT.		
Oct. 4	Birch	Salford	7		
,, 11	Widnes	Salford	2		
,, 18	Oldham	Oldham	2		
,, 25	Birch	Birch	1		
Nov. 1	Broughton Rangers	Salford			1
,, 8	Swinton	Salford			1
,, 15	Bradford	Bradford	1	3	4
,, 22	Widnes	Widnes	2	1	
,, 29	Halifax	Salford		2	4
Dec. 6	Rochdale Hornets	Rochdale		2	
,, 13	Walton	Walton	0		
,, 20	Stoke-on-Trent	Stoke	3	3	
,, 27	Halifax	Halifax			2
1885.					
Jan. 3	Free Wanderers	Fallowfield			
,, 10	Walton	Salford	3	2	1
,, 17	Cheetham	Cheetham		3	
,, 24	Oldham	Salford			
,, 31	Bradford	Salford			2
Feb. 7	Dewsbury	Salford	4	1	1
,, 14	Free Wanderers	Salford	1	4	1
,, 21	Rochdale Hornets	Salford	1	4	
,, 28	Cheetham	Salford		3	
Mar. 7	Askam	Salford	1	2	
,, 14	Swinton	Swinton	0		
,, 21	Broughton Rangers	Broughton rv.		2	2
,, 28	Dewsbury	Dewsbury			
Apr. 4	Barrow	Barrow		1	
	Askam	Askam	0		

A member's ground admission card for the 1884/85 season. During a purple patch the team lost just 6 of 27 matches played. This was Salford's seventh season at their New Barnes enclosure, adjacent to the Salford-based Manchester Racecourse that covered the length of Trafford Road.

This picture, taken in New Zealand in late Spring 1888, shows the historic first touring party in their red, blue and white hooped jerseys. It includes four Salford players: Jack Anderton, Sam Williams, Harry Eagles and Tom Kent. All the players in the party are included in this picture. From left to right, back row: Banks (Swinton), Stoddart (Blackheath), Clowes (Halifax), Lawlor (supporter), Smith (Edinburgh Univ.), Paul (Swinton), McShane (supporter). Middle row: Anderton, Penketh (Douglas), Williams, R. Burnett (Hawick), Thomas (Cambridge Univ.), Seddon (Swinton), Eagles, Kent, Mathers (Bramley). Front row: Speakman (Runcorn), W. Burnett (Hawick), Brooks (Edinburgh Univ.), Bumby (Swinton), Haslam (Batley), Nolan (Rochdale), Stuart (Dewsbury), Laing (Hawick).

Team line-up for the 1888/89 season. From left to right, back row: J. Horrocks (vice-president), James Higson (honorary secretary), Jack Anderton, T.J. Smith, Jack Roberts, J. McVittie, Sam Williams, Arthur Smith, D. Wellwood (chairman), S. Whiteley (honorary treasurer). Middle row: Robert Walmsley (umpire), Ted Austin, William Manwaring, J. Mallinson, Alf Barrett, Tom King, A. Foster. Front row: J. Newton, H.H. Clegg, Harry Eagles (captain), Herbert Cook, Joe Shaw. The club played 40 matches during the season and, after winning only three of the first nine (prior to the return of their four tourists in mid-November), they lost only six more.

Salford transferred their headquarters to the London and North Western Hotel in nearby Cross Lane from the 1888/89 season. This advertisement appeared in James Higson's *History of the Salford Football Club* published in 1892.

The programme card for the game against the touring Maori side on 16 March 1889. Played at New Barnes, it attracted over 10,000 spectators to the ground, with gate reciepts of £144. The tourists won by 2 goals and a try (7 points) to a try (1 point) in a match that was contested in pouring rain. Salford also played for much of the game with fourteen players after try scorer H.H. Clegg was injured. The weather conditions were seen as an advantage for the visitors over a lighter Salford pack as, even in those days, Salford had built a reputation for mobility and running the ball. Officially called the New Zealand Native Football Representatives, their match against Salford was the sixty-ninth in a mammoth seventy-four game schedule.

Go ye forward in your might,
Strive with all your heart and soul,
Stand forth—Champions in the fight,
Aim at nothing but the goal.
We are of one flesh and blood,
We are of one brotherhood.—A. C.

MAORIS v. SALFORD

At Salford, March 16th, 1889.

MAORIS.

Full Back.—D. GAGE.

Three-Quarter Backs.

M'CAUSLAND.   W. WYNYARD.   F. WARBRICK.

Half-Backs.

ELLIOT.   H. WYNYARD.   SMILER.

Forwards.

ELLISON.   TAIAROA.   H. LEE.   WILLIAMS.
A. WARBRICK.   ANDERSON.   MAYNARD.
STEWART.

SALFORD.

Full Back.—MAINWARING.

Three-Quarter Backs.

ANDERTON.   BARRETT.   COOK.

Half-Backs.

NEWTON.   CLEGG.

Forwards.

EAGLES.   ROBERTS.   WILLIAMS.
JOHNSON.   AUSTIN.   KING.   McVITTIE
A. SMITH.   SHAW.

J.W. (Jack) Roberts was the Salford vice-captain for the match against the Maori touring side in 1888. His total of 271 appearances (1883-1895) and 100 tries for Salford place him second on both lists during the club's Rugby Union era. His playing days for Salford spanned thirteen seasons – the longest by any player during the Rugby Union period. He was capped 4 times by Lancashire between 1887 and 1889.

At 5ft 5ins, William Manwaring was small in stature and affectionately referred to as 'Little Manwaring'. He was to make the full-back slot his own, however, during eleven illustrious seasons at the club. His 276 appearances, beginning in 1886, is a Salford record as members of the Rugby Union (to which he added 24 more under the auspices of the Northern Union). He also made 9 Lancashire county appearances during the 1890s.

Centre three-quarter Alf Barrett was a model of consistency during his seven seasons at the club barely missing a match. From his home debut against Bradford in October 1888, he only failed to appear in 12 matches for Salford before 1895, and that was partly due to his 10 county appearances for Lancashire during that period. In all, he played 223 times for Salford, contributing 47 tries and 9 goals.

The Salford team in 1890/91. From left to right, back row: H.H. Clegg (umpire), Tom Kent, J. Birch, J. McVittie, Jack Tune, Frank Knowles, Joe Shaw, S. Whiteley (honorary treasurer). Middle row (seated): J. Horrocks (vice-chairman), Alf Barrett, Jack Roberts, Frank Miles, D. Wellworth (chairman), Harry Eagles (captain), E. Barrett, Tom King, James Higson (honorary secretary). Front row (on floor): G.H. Tonge, Sam Walch. This side lost just 11 of the 35 matches played during the campaign.

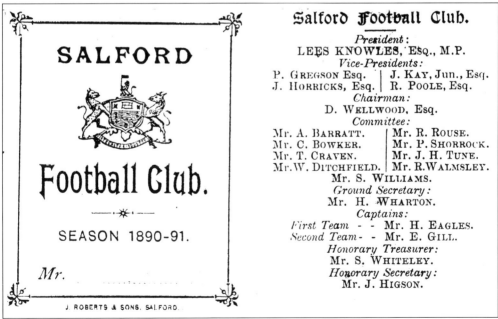

A membership card from 1890/91; this was one of over 2,100 that were to be issued that season. Salford was now a formidable outfit with two internationals and eight county players in the team and spectator interest was growing rapidly. The fans would be rewarded when Salford became the first team to win the new Lancashire Club Championship in the 1892/93 season.

Tom Kent earned the distinction of being the only player from the Salford club to actually play for the England Rugby Union team. Described as a solid, hard-working forward, he was selected 6 times for England during 1891 and 1892, having already contributed to the 1888 tour of Australia and New Zealand. His consistent form is well illustrated by his 32 Lancashire county appearances between 1888 and 1893, a record for a Salford player under any code of rugby. He also played three times in the North versus South match between 1887 and 1890, thus becoming one of only three players from the club to be selected. His career at Salford began in 1887 and he made 169 appearances.

Sam Walch first played for Salford in October 1889, having previously been with local rivals Swinton. A half-back who was noted for his defensive qualities, he made 164 appearances for the club under both Rugby Union and Northern Union rules. He was also capped for Lancashire twice, against Durham in 1893 and the Midland Counties in 1894.

V.J. (Victor) Slater proved to be a sensational capture for the club from Ardwick, making a try-scoring debut in the win at Widnes in November 1884. He was a gifted centre three-quarter, probably the best the club had during the Rugby Union period. Over four seasons he scored 14 tries and 18 goals before suffering what was, effectively, a career-ending injury at Dewsbury in October 1887. Although he returned for a handful of matches before the end of that season, he never recovered properly and retired from the game. A prominent touch kicker, he played 6 times for Lancashire in 1886 and 1887.

Salford had several good wing three-quarters during this period. Teenage speedster Frank Miles proved to be a ready-made replacement for the 1888 tourist, Jack Anderton, when the latter left the club in 1889. Described, somewhat poetically, as a winger with 'a swiftness that defied pursuit', his pace and elusiveness was a sharp contrast to the powerful direct running style of Anderton. Born in nearby Eccles in 1871 and signed from the Barton club, he made his first appearance for Salford in the home match against Rochdale Hornets in September 1889. He proved to be the club's first superstar, topping the team try-scoring list for five consecutive seasons and twice setting a club record for the most tries in a season. In total, he scored 128 tries in 180 matches with his 27 touchdowns in 1890/91 being particularly impressive for the era. His six tries against Oldham junior side, Lees, in the Northern Union Cup in March 1898, set a club record that has been equalled twice but never beaten. In one match, against Runcorn on 1 February 1890, he scored three tries in only five minutes, a feat repeated by David Watkins on 1 December 1972 against Barrow at The Willows. He was the first victorious Salford captain when the Lancashire Club Championship was secured in 1892/93 and he played 5 times for Lancashire between 1890 and 1892.

SALFORD FOOTBALL CLUB.

REPORT AND BALANCE SHEET,

For presentation at ANNUAL MEETING, JUNE 1st, 1892.

THE Committee have pleasure in submitting to the Members their Report and Balance Sheet for the Season 1891-92. The First Team, owing to the numerous changes and lack of combination at the beginning of the season, have not done so well as in previous seasons, 35 matches having been played—18 won, 13 lost, and 4 drawn.

The points scored are:—

	GOALS.		TRIES.		POINTS.
Salford	24	....	50	or	218
Opponents	22	....	37	or	180
	2		13	or	38 points in favour of the Club.

The "A" Team have an excellent record, considering the calls made upon their players to supply vacancies on the First Team, having played 26 matches—won 17, lost 5, drawn 4.

Salford "A"	32				
Opponents	14	....	15	or	99
	18		50	or	183 points in favour of "A" Team.

Three of this season's team have been called upon to play for the County (Messrs. Craven, Kent, and Miles). Kent, although passed over by the northern portion of the Rugby Union Committee for the North *v.* South match, has had the honour to be chosen and play in the three International fixtures.

The erection of a Covered Stand, hoarding round the ground, and other improvements has caused an adverse balance to appear on the season's working.

Next season's engagements will be found to contain new fixtures with St. Helen's Recreation, renewed fixtures with Warrington and Oldham, and the disappearance of Newport, Swansea, and Burton.

A Challenge Shield (presented by our President, LEES KNOWLES, Esq., M.P.) and 30 Silver Medals, presented by the Club, have been offered for competition amongst the junior clubs in the County Borough of Salford, the first winners being the Rainsough team.

The Committee have also decided to endow a Bed at the Salford Royal Hospital, out of the proceeds of the gate moneys received from the Challenge Shield matches, at an annual subscription of £50.

The number of Tickets issued has been: Honorary and Playing, 1,362; Subscribers, 51; Youths', 160; Total, 1573.

JAMES HIGSON,

HON. SECRETARY.

The report and balance sheet for the 1891/92 season indicates that results were disappointing compared to previous campaigns, despite the claim that only 13 matches were lost from 35 played. The report overlooked three games as Salford actually lost 14 from 38, with the dependable Harry Eagles appearing in all of them. It was the highest number of defeats suffered in a season since the name of Salford Football Club was adopted in 1879. The new covered stand, referred to in the report, was opened in November 1891, although a section of it blew down in a gale a few months later. It was soon repaired and the 2,000 spectators it accommodated brought the capacity of the New Barnes ground up to 15,000.

James Higson was one of the most influential figures at the club during this period. As the honorary secretary of the Crescent club, he played a major role in bringing about the merger with Salford in 1881. He took on a similar position with Salford in 1886 after serving two seasons as assistant secretary and another as treasurer. He also became the first Salford representative on the Lancashire county committee in 1886. In 1892 he had the foresight to write an invaluable early history of the club, a book that can now be seen as being ahead of its time. In 1896, as covered in the following chapter, he was to be a controversial figure in Salford's eventual breakaway from the English Rugby Union.

The Lancashire team prior to the match against Cheshire at Swinton on 2 November 1895. From left to right, back row: L.E. Pilkington (St Helens Recs), Richard Pierce (Liverpool), S. Walsh (Pemberton), John Pinch (Lancaster), J. Jones (Salford), W. Parlane (Manchester), A.M. Crook (honorary secretary). Middle row: R. Holmes (Morecambe), Wilfred Stoddart (Liverpool), George Hughes (Barrow), Harold Murray (Swinton), Jim Valentine (Swinton, captain), Jack Lewis (Swinton), Robert Moss (Salford), F.A. Grover (vice-president). Front row: G.G. Allen (Liverpool), William Manwaring (Salford). Lancashire won 23-3. This was the first match played by the Lancashire Rugby Union team after the great split and the selection illustrates the isolation of senior clubs Salford and Swinton in not joining the Northern Union the previous August. Salford's decision was surprising as the club was banned for several months over alleged professionalism at the end of 1894. This occurred after Salford signed Radcliffe three-quarter Joe Smith. The Radcliffe club subsequently accused Salford of luring him away with payments of 35 shillings (£1.75p) per week, a view upheld by the Lancashire committee. The three Salford players (Jones, Manwaring and Moss) all played for Salford in the Northern Union the following season.

Two
Salford Join the Rebels
1896-1914

Salford made an early impression in the Northern Union following the momentous decision to resign from the English Rugby Football Union in 1896. Over the next ten seasons the team appeared in four Northern Union Challenge Cup finals (now known as the Rugby League Challenge Cup), and was championship runners-up for three consecutive seasons. In 1901, the club set a transfer record when they tempted Jimmy Lomas to leave Bramley for £100, that figure being decided by a tribunal. Lomas was worth every penny as he was destined to become a legendary figure in the game. This picture shows Lomas winning a goal-kicking competition against the Australian captain Dally Messenger, prior to the first Test match at the Royal Agricultural Showground in Sydney on 18 June 1910. It was the Northern Union's first ever tour of Australasia and Lomas was chosen as the tour captain, the first of three Salford players to be honoured in this way.

FOOTBALL.

SPECIAL MEETING OF THE SALFORD CLUB.

A special general meeting of the Salford Football Club was held on Thursday evening in Hope Board School, Liverpool-street, Salford. Dr. W. B. Smith, who presided, was supported on the platform by Messrs. T. Greenhalgh, J. R. Dobson, T. L. Brinelow, and W. Mainwaring. There were about 400 present. The meeting was called in compliance with a requisition signed by 89 members of the club for the purpose of discussing the desirability or otherwise of joining the Northern Union. Our representative presented himself at the meeting, but was refused admittance. We learn that after the notice convening the meeting had been read, the Chairman called upon Mr. Daniels to propose a resolution to the effect that Salford apply for membership in the Northern Union.—Councillor Higson asked if all the members present had paid their subscriptions?—Mr. R. Walmsley said the players had been admitted but they were as much members as Mr. Higson himself.—Mr. Isaac Hall asked whether Mr. Higson was in possession of a ticket; if not he had no right there.—Councillor Higson said Mr. Walmsley had been in possession of his subscription some few days now.—Mr. Walmsley confirmed this. — Mr. J. Daniels proposed the resolution. He said pure amateurism was played out, and as Salford was a working-class club and didn't contain any so-called gentlemen, he considered it would be very nice for the players to have a present of 6s. worth of silver every week—(laughter). If they continued on amateur lines it simply meant that they would go to smash. They all knew working-class clubs were better supported than such clubs as Liverpool and Manchester.—Mr. W. Rouse seconded the resolution without making any remarks.—Councillor Higson congratulated the mover on the fair way in which he had proposed the resolution. He thought the resolution savoured of the inspiration of the committee, for they had it on the authority of Mr. Walmsley that the committee had discussed the advisability of joining the Northern Union and had unanimously decided to apply for membership. He called attention to the last two general meetings held by the club, when a resolution was carried unanimously that the committee should act up to and abide by the laws of the Rugby Union, and he asked whether the committee had carried out those instructions. If they had not what was the reason? Secondly, had the committee instructed a certain member to attend the meetings of the Northern Union to apply for membership? He thought the committee would do anything at the present moment. What had put the club in its present position? He could unhesitatingly reply that a committee-man who obtained his place on the committee, not because he had played football, nor because he knew anything about the game, but simply because he had an ambition to be a light in the football world, was the cause of a lot of bother. These men mixed with popular players and got them to support their candidature, on the understanding that they would be subsequently well paid for it. Thus it was that players made repeated applications for higher payments, and when once the committee had got itself into trouble they had to go on doing wrong. During the past four years the Salford Club had lost £713 13s. 11d., so that it was no wonder some of their former friends were heartily sick of the unbusinesslike way in which things were conducted. Nothing but insults had been heaped upon officials who had dared to say football could be played as an amateur sport. They knew very well that the Northern Union was formed to fight the Salford Football Club when it was suspended for professionalism. With regard to the payment for "broken time," that was simply a myth. Mr. Higson said several of the clubs that had joined the Northern Union were financially worse off than before. If the Salford committee thought that by joining the union they could get better players he thought they were making a mistake. In a speech lasting over half-an-hour, during which he was frequently interrupted, Mr. Higson strongly condemned the proposal.—Mr. D. Jones, while partly agreeing with what Mr. Higson had said, spoke in favour of joining the union.—Mr. Walmsley said if they didn't join the union there was nothing for them but ruin.—Mr. S. Boswell supported Councillor Higson.—The resolution was carried, there being only three dissentients.

ST. PAUL'S BAZAAR, PENDLETON.

OPENING CEREMONIES.

For some months past the members of St. Paul's Church, Ellor-street, Pendleton, have been anxiously looking forward to the time when they might make a tangible effort to clear off the existing debt caused by the recent restoration of the church. Those hopes were realised on Thursday afternoon, when a three days' bazaar, in the school-room, Ellor-street, was opened by the Mayor of Salford (Alderman R. Mottram, J.P.). Anyone acquainted with St. Paul's Church two or three years ago, and casually visiting it now would scarcely recognise that it was the same place of worship, so marked are the internal improvements which have been effected. When the Rev. T. Edelston was appointed vicar a little more than twelve months ago, he at once saw the necessity for taking immediate steps to re-roof the church, and carry out other repairs and alterations urgently required. This was by no means an easy matter, as the congregation was comparatively small, and consisted of the artizans class. The new vicar, however, soon got round him a number of devoted and enthusiastic workers, who were anxious to render assistance in the worthy object of restoring their church. Matters were quickly arranged, and before the end of the year the much needed work had been done at a cost of about £700. By means of subscriptions, &c., upwards of half the amount required has already been raised. It is hoped that at the conclusion of the bazaar the funds will find that the debt, if not extinguished, has been considerably reduced. Unfortunately the rain descended in torrents just at the time fixed for the opening ceremony. Notwithstanding this fact, however, there was a large number of friends present. The room had been made bright and attractive by the use of curtains, bunting, flowers, &c. The Vicar presided, and was supported by the Mayor (wearing his chain of office), the Mayoress and Miss Mottram, Mrs. Edelston, the Rev. R. Coverdale, curate of St. George's Church, Charlestown, and Mr. Hugh Cecil Birley. Amongst those in the body of the hall were Mrs. Wood (Bolton-road), Mr. and Mrs. Hall (Seedley), Mrs. Hall, Misses Hall and Mr. Harry Hall (Broad-street),

When most of the senior northern clubs left the Rugby Union in August 1895, James Higson had encouraged Salford to remain loyal and was cheered by the members for his stance. Twelve months later he found himself at the centre of a historic, but stormy, meeting at the Hope Board School in Liverpool Street on 16 April 1896. At this meeting, the members voted to resign from the English RFU and apply for Northern Union membership, with Higson virtually alone in opposing the motion. *The Salford Reporter*'s account of the proceedings show that Higson was the central figure in a hostile meeting. The Lancashire county committee formerly accepted the club's resignation when they met at Manchester's Grand Hotel on 9 June 1896. Higson subsequently broke all ties with Salford and became honorary secretary of the Lancashire RFU. He remained a strong critic of the Northern Union, but the wound healed and he returned to Salford several years later.

LIST OF FIXTURES, 1896-97.

FIRST TEAM.

Date.	Club.	Gr'nd.
1896.		
Sept. 5	Widnes	Away
" 12	Oldham	Home
" 19	St. Helens	Home
" 26	Leigh	Away
Oct. 3	Rochdale Hornets	Home
" 10	Stockport	Away
" 12*	Brighouse Rangers	Away
" 17	Warrington	Away
" 24	Swinton	Away
" 31	Broughton Rangers	Away
Nov. 7	Wigan	Home
" 14	Tyldesley	Away
" 21	Walkden	Away
" 28	St. Clement's	Home
Dec. 5	Morecambe	Home
" 12	Runcorn	Home
" 19	Oldham	Away
" 25	Christmas Day.	
" 26	Tyldesley	Home
1897.		
Jan. 1	Wigan	Away
" 2	Morecambe	Away
" 4*	Huddersfield	Home
" 9	Rochdale Hornets	Away
" 16	Runcorn	Away
" 23	Widnes	Home
" 30	St. Helens	Away
Feb. 6	Stockport	Home
" 13	Swinton	Home
" 20	Walkden	Home
" 27	Broughton Rangers	Home
Mar. 6	Warrington	Home
" 13	Leigh	Home
" 20	Cup Ties	
" 27		
Apl. 3		
" 10		
" 16†	Manningham	Away
" 17	Manningham	Home
" 19‡	Brighouse Rangers	Home
" 20§	Huddersfield	Away
" 24	St. Clement's	Away

"A" TEAM.

Date.	Club.	Gr'nd.
1896.		
Sept. 5	Widnes	Home
" 12	Oldham	Away
" 19	St. Helens	Away
" 26	Leigh	Home
Oct. 3	Rochdale Hornets	Away
" 10	Stockport	Home
" 17	Warrington	Home
" 24	Swinton	Home
" 31	Broughton Rangers	Home
Nov. 7	Wigan	Away
" 14	Tyldesley	Home
" 21	Stockport Rangers	Home
" 28	St. Clement's	Away
Dec. 5	Werneth	Away
" 12	Runcorn	Away
" 19	Oldham	Home
" 25	Christmas Day.	
" 26	Tyldesley	Away
1897.		
Jan. 1	Wigan	Home
" 2	Werneth	Home
" 9	Rochdale Hornets	Home
" 16	Runcorn	Home
" 23	St. Helens	Away
" 30	St. Helens	Home
Feb. 6	Stockport	Away
" 13	Swinton	Away
" 20	Dukinfield	Away
" 27	Broughton Rangers	Away
Mar. 6	Warrington	Away
" 13	Leigh	Away
" 20		
" 27		
Apl. 3		
" 10	Stockport Rangers	Away
" 16†	Dukinfield	Home
" 17		
" 19‡		
" 20§		
" 24	St. Clement's	Home

* Monday Matches. † Good Friday. ‡ Easter Monday. § Easter Tuesday.

A member's fixture card for 1896/97, Salford's historic first season in the Northern Union. It includes the famous Swinton centre, Jim Valentine, as the team captain. Valentine, with 4 England caps and countless appearances for Lancashire, was considered a major capture and unanimously elected captain for the new season at the committee meeting on 8 August 1896. Swinton tried desperately to keep their prized asset but he stated in the press that he was determined to play for Salford, a club he had guested for on four previous occasions. On the eve of the opening match, however, he surprisingly reversed his decision and remained with Swinton. Salford were embarrassingly left with Valentine on their membership cards.

In the early years, Salford and Broughton Rangers had a joint match programme that they shared with their soccer cousins at Newton Heath and Manchester City. Newton Heath, members of the Football League at the time, changed their name to Manchester United in 1902.

The Manchester Racecourse in the late 1890s with the new ship canal in the foreground. Although barely visible, Salford's New Barnes ground is in the top left behind the stands. The No. 9 dock of the Manchester Ship Canal was the final piece in the dockland jigsaw when it opened in 1905. Unfortunately, the land it was built on included New Barnes, the home of the Salford club for twenty-two seasons. Along with the adjoining racecourse, they were given notice to quit the site, without warning, in the middle of the 1900/01 season. It was reported as 'a time of great anxiety for the club with limited funding available to obtain a new ground'. Salford's directors appealed for more time to find a new home, which was granted and, eventually, they obtained land at the Willows Estate, situated in the Weaste district of Salford. At their meeting on 8 February 1901, the club confirmed the move and agreed that a limited company should be created to raise the capital required.

Salford made their debut at the new ground, known today as The Willows, on 21 December 1901 against traditional rivals Swinton. Several VIPs were invited to the match, including the mayor and local MPs, and they were entertained, along with the record crowd of 16,981, by the South Salford Band before the kick-off. The team posed for this picture at the ground, prior to the match. Jimmy Lomas (front row, extreme left) kicked the only goal in a 2-0 victory. The Salford line-up for this historic match was: Smith; Bone, T. Williams, Varty, Price; Lomas, Griffiths; Brown, H. Buckler, Heath, Rhapps, Shaw, Shore, Tunney, J. Williams. Salford appeared in their second Northern Union Challenge Cup final at the end of the season, but lost by 25-0 to Broughton Rangers. The previous final had also been unsuccessful, losing to Swinton by 16-8 in 1900.

The ambitious move to The Willows ground was a huge drain on club funds and an appeal went out for more financial backing. One enterprise was the staging of a four-day bazaar at the Grove Lads' Club in Salford's Regent Road during March 1903. As can be seen in this extract from the eighty-four-page bazaar brochure, the target was to raise £2,000 towards the cycle track that would later surround the pitch. In fact the bazaar, which was well supported by local dignitaries, who made grand opening speeches prior to each day, raised £600 after the deduction of running costs. The cycle track lasted until the early 1930s, when it was removed for terrace expansion.

BRITISH SPORTS ✤ ✤ ✤

Objects of the Bazaar

✤ ✤

✤

His Bazaar is being held with the object of raising the sum of £2,000 to place the Club in a thoroughly sound financial position. It may be of interest to those who are not members, but who are lovers of the sport, to know that about £3,000 has already been expended in laying out the New Ground at Weaste, and providing stand accommodation for upwards of 12,000 people. A further sum is required to complete the Cycling Track and the banking-up of the corners of the ground, which, when completed, will make the enclosure undoubtedly the finest in Lancashire.

For about a quarter of a century the Club has had an active and honourable career, having provided healthy recreation and enjoyment for many thousands, and has been the means of raising and contributing many hundreds of pounds to deserving institutions, among which may be mentioned :—Salford Royal Hospital, Children's Hospital, Nurses' Home, Cinderella Club, South African War Fund, and has assisted in raising money for the Lancashire Fusilier Compassionate Fund. It has also rendered monetary assistance to Junior Football and Cricket Clubs.

The Club having fully justified its existence in the Borough, we earnestly appeal to you for support and respectfully ask you to kindly interest yourself in the Bazaar and to render any assistance in your power.

Salford played in their third Northern Union Challenge Cup final at Headingley, in 1903. Here, Salford skipper Jimmy Lomas (right) watches as Halifax captain Archie Rigg tosses a coin before the match. Halifax won 7-0 in front of a record cup final crowd of 32,506, an attendance that was not beaten until the 1922 final.

The Salford team for the 1904/05 season. From left to right, back row: E. Mather (chairman), J. Graham, Jack Williams, Jack Rhapps, Dai Rees, Pat Tunney, Robert Shaw, S. Bebbington, George Cooke (trainer). Middle row (seated except where stated): George Heath (kneeling), Willie Thomas, Jimmy Lomas (captain), Arthur Bedford, R.B. Parry, William Brown, A. Norris, Ike Lewis (kneeling). Front row (on ground): R. Richards, Dave Preston, E.T. Harter, William Lambert. Having finished runners-up in the championship in each of the three previous campaigns, Salford slipped back to sixth place during the season. The previous year had been quite an eventful one. After finishing level with Bradford at the top of the championship table, it was agreed that the two clubs should meet in a decider at Halifax. Salford lost 5-0 in front of 12,000 spectators. This was, in effect, the first ever championship final as the play-off system, initially contested by the top four teams, was not formally introduced until the 1906/07 season. The Willows had also hosted the Northern Union Challenge Cup final for the first time on 30 April 1904, when 17,041 watched as Halifax defeated Warrington 8-3.

Salford 1905/06. From left to right, back row: Brown, Williams, Rhapps, E. Thomas, Warwick, Rees, John (small chap in civvies). Middle row: Cochrane, Bell, W. Thomas, Lomas (captain), Hampson, Lewis, Preston. Front row: Holbrook, H. Buckler, A. Buckler. This was a photocall in April 1906, prior to the Northern Union Challenge Cup final against Bradford at Headingley later in the month. Dai John, injured at the time, could almost be mistaken for a ball boy. Appearances can be deceptive as the tiny Welshman, noted for his speed and elusiveness, played 406 matches for Salford from 1905 to 1922. This total would have been even more if the First World War hadn't interrupted his career. As it was, he played a further 49 wartime friendly games between 1915 and 1917.

Caricatures for the 1906 Northern Union Challenge Cup final featuring players from both teams. The three Salford players are half-back Dave Preston (256 appearances 1902-1913), Welsh forward Evan Thomas (307 appearances 1905-1915) and skipper Jimmy Lomas. It was Salford's fourth final in seven seasons but, like the previous three, the team finished runners-up. The 5-0 Bradford victory meant the Reds failed to score in their third successive final! This season was also the last played with teams of fifteen. At the Northern Union AGM on 12 June 1906, it was agreed to drop two of the forwards, thus introducing the thirteen-a-side game familiar to modern Rugby League supporters.

Jimmy Lomas, seen wearing his England jersey in this autographed picture, is recalled in Rugby League folklore as the first British tour captain. At Salford, he is remembered as a match winning stand-off or centre who seemingly set new milestones each season. It took a new record transfer fee of £100 to secure him, when signed from Bramley in 1901, that stood until broken by Lomas himself in January 1911, when he moved to Oldham for £300. Pictures of Lomas clearly illustrate his stocky build and it was this upper body strength, combined with his shortness (5ft 7in) that made him so difficult to bring down. Lomas played 312 times for Salford, scored 210 tries and kicked 470 goals. He is the fourth highest try scorer in the club's history, the third highest goal scorer and the third highest point scorer. His 39 points against Liverpool City in 1907 stood as the Rugby League record for a league championship fixture until Dean Marwood of Workington Town scored 42 points against Highfield in 1992. He was Salford's top try scorer for nine consecutive seasons and the leading goal scorer for ten. Amazingly, his career with Salford spanned twenty-two years. Despite four major finals, he failed to win any honours with Salford, a situation that was rectified after his transfer to Oldham. He gained representative honours with Great Britain, England, Lancashire and his native county, Cumberland. After leaving in 1911 he made two comebacks with Salford – three wartime friendly matches in 1917 and then a further eight appearances during 1923.

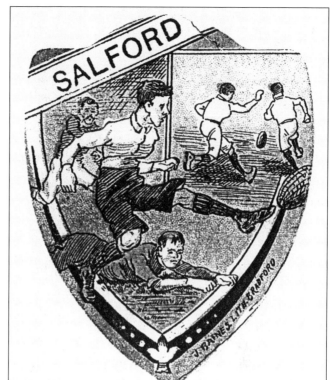

Baines cards first appeared during the 1880s and were produced up to the First World War. The brainchild of John Baines of Bradford, they were sold in packets of six and proved very popular amongst the younger supporters of the day. All the cards were printed in colour. On this page are just two examples from the many that featured Salford.

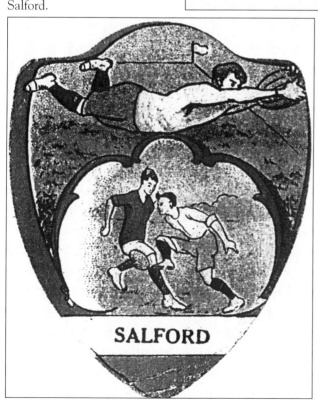

The Salford team before meeting Leeds in a third round Northern Union Challenge cup clash at The Willows on 30 March 1907. From left to right, back row: Joe White (trainer), W. Brady, Alf Foster, Ike Lewis, Evan Thomas, Silas Warwick, Dai Rees, William Lambert (assistant trainer), John Cochrane. Middle row: Arthur Buckler, Charlie Garner, Willie Thomas, Jimmy Lomas (captain), Vernon Hampson, Albert Mason, William Brown. Front row (on ground): Dai John, Dave Preston. Brady and Foster were non-playing reserves. Although not kitted out for this particular match due to injury, Cochrane played 29 times during the season. Salford won the tie 12-3 to earn a semi-final place. The Reds failed to progress to the final, however, losing 6-0 to Oldham at Rochdale. During the season, Lomas set new club records for tries (34), goals (82) and points (266). All three figures were to stand for over a quarter of a century until the arrival of Lance Todd's famous Red Devils of the 1930s.

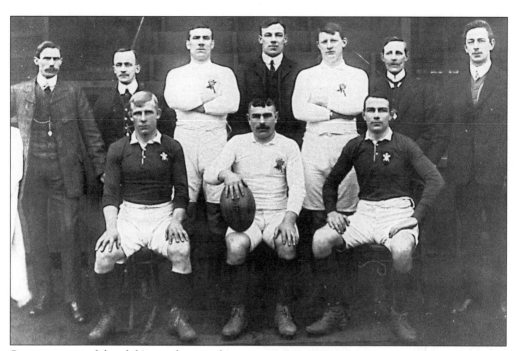

Some measure of the club's standing can be gauged from this photograph, taken around 1909, featuring six of the team's international stars. From left to right, back row: J. White (trainer), J.P. Stoddard (director), J. Spencer (England), E. Thomas (Wales), S. Warwick (England), F.P. Crowshaw (director), V. Wright (secretary). Front row: H. Buckler (Wales), J. Lomas (England), D. Rees (Wales). The first match between England and Wales took place at Tonypandy on 20 April 1908, with Wales winning 35-18. The clash became an annual affair and further matches were organised for the two countries against the Australian and New Zealand tourists.

Welsh centre Willie Thomas first played for Salford in 1903 after signing from Aberavon Rugby Union Club. He played 444 times for Salford, a figure only bettered by two other players. He also took part in 57 wartime friendly matches. The crowning moment of his career was, without doubt, when he captained Salford to the 1914 Championship. He ended his Salford career on a high note, scoring a try against the Australian tourists in 1921. This picture appeared in the Pinnace collection of 1923 (see next chapter).

W. THOMAS

461 SALFORD. N.U.

The Salford players and officials with their first major trophy, having been acclaimed as Northern Rugby League Champions for 1913/14. From left to right, back row: W. Tomkinson, J.P. Knowles, G. Trafford, S. Daber, G.C. Swire (chairman), T. Gaskell, George S. Cadman, Joe White (trainer). Third row: Harry Goldsmith, Charlie Rees, George Currie, Evan Thomas, Bob Ritchie, Ernie Woods, Jack Bevon, George Thom. Second row (seated except where stated): J.P. Stoddard (standing), Walter Clegg, George Callender, Willie Thomas (captain), Arthur Loveluck, Bernard Mesley, Harry Launce, V. Wright (secretary-manager, seated on

stool). Front row: A.H.R. Holt (kneeling), Dai John (vice-captain), Edgar May, H.E. Roberts (kneeling). Salford's narrow 5-3 success over Huddersfield in the final at Headingley was unexpected as their opponents were considered to be the greatest team ever seen in the Northern Union up to that time. Salford had fought back after the Yorkshire side had taken the lead and resisted terrific pressure in the second half. Willie Thomas said later: 'If we felt proud at the moment of victory when we knew we had beaten the great Huddersfield side, we felt prouder still when we got back to Salford and found such a welcome awaiting us.'

Captain Jimmy Lomas with his team before the first Northern Union tour match ever played. From left to right, back row: Tom 'Chick' Jenkins (Ebbw Vale), Billy Winstanley (Leigh), Dick Ramsdale (Wigan), George Ruddick (Broughton Rangers), Johnny Thomas (Wigan). Middle row: Frank Young (Leeds), Billy Jukes (Hunslet), Jimmy Lomas (Salford, captain), Frank Boylen (Hull), John Bartholomew (Huddersfield). Front row (on ground): Fred Webster (Leeds), Fred Farrar (Hunslet), Fred Smith (Hunslet). Played at the Sydney Agricultural Showground on 4 June 1910, the tourists lost 28-14 to New South Wales, although Lomas could at least claim the first points of the tour with a penalty goal. The match was watched by a 37,000 crowd, eager to get their first glimpse of the visitors. The tourists won the Test series against Australia and were successful in a one-off match against New Zealand in Wellington. Salford forward Ephraim Curzon was also a member of the tour party, although not featured in this picture.

Three
The 3,000 Mugs
1915-1927

After winning the championship in 1914, Salford's fortunes went into decline. That success had been won with the threat of extinction hanging over the club and, in fact, the official receiver had been called in during 1912, resulting in Salford being managed by a special advisory committee. Eventually, in August 1914, it was announced that a new company, entitled 'Salford Football Club (1914) Limited', had been formed, which continues today. The off-field difficulties were reflected in the performance of the team, who struggled through the wartime friendly games and continued to do so in the post-war years. The 1920s era is a particularly low point in the history of the Salford club and even the supporters called themselves 'The 3,000 Mugs'. This team picture, taken at The Willows during the 1926/27 season, shows captain Jack Gore (middle row, with ball) sandwiched between club chairman and former top referee, J. Priestley (to his right), and the talented Cumbrian player Fergie Southward. From this season the team represented the City of Salford, the previous status of Royal Borough having been superseded in April 1926.

GROVES & WI

Famous

Salford

We had two very interesting visitors at the match with Swinton on Boxing Day—Serjeant Billy Brady and Bombardier Wilson, both taking a little respite from active service. They looked remarkably well, indeed, Billy was anxious to know if there was a chance for him to turn out. Bombr. Wilson came to the offices after the match to give a special message of thanks from himself and comrades to everyone connected with the Club, for the newspapers, sweets, tobacco, &c. sent out to them. He hopes that he may be able to return the football after the war as a souvenir.

At last we have news of George Callender, and we are sure everyone will be pleased to hear that all is well with him. It appears that George has been moved about a good bit and this will account for the previous absence of news. He is now with the Mediterranean Expeditionary Force and tells us that the football we sent him is still fit and provides endless recreation for himself and his pals.

Grand Matc

Saturday, January

Kick-

The First World War meant that most players were away fighting for King and Country, many never to return. The majority of clubs continued to play a full set of friendly fixtures, albeit with a mix of juniors, old heads and guests making up their teams. The Salford programmes produced for matches played during the war were basic, but informative, particularly with regard to the war effort itself. This one, for the clash with Leigh on 8 January 1916, gave details of players on

Leigh.

1916. Kick-off 2-45 p.m.

LEIGH (Red and White Jerseys)

Selected from—

. Clarkson	Full Back
'Nell	Right Wing
igham	Right Centre
eegan	Left Centre
rundy	Left Wing
arter	Outside
Tooney	Scrum
arwell	Forward
avies	,,
oardman	,,
. Cartwright	,,
Marsh	,,
. Shaw	,,
ent	,,
aln	,,
Vhalley	,,

(Numbers have not been supplied)

rs. Chapman (Swnt'n)& Lowe(Brou'ton)

---

t Salford :

alford. v Dewsbury.

p m.

We have been rather severely hit by injuries to players during the last few weeks. Arthur Loveluck was damaged in the Runcorn match, and was unable to take part in the holiday matches, but we hope he will be fit for to-day. Charlie Rees got his shoulder damaged on Xmas Day, and Sykes dislocated his thumb on New Year's Day—both are in the Doctor's hands. Tom Coates has had to suffering from appendicitis. We are glad to say the last reports state the operation has been successful and that Tom is doing well.

In the list of players from which to-day's team will be selected appears the name of F. Gagon. This is a local lad and is said to be a capable one and a fast runner. We have also signed J. Gould—full back or three-quarter—who played in junior football with a Yorkshire Club—Leeds Star.

Shakespeare wrote—"Let him not pass but kill him rather."—One could almost imagine the Bard had just returned from a Rugby " Derby " when he penned those lines.

The amount collected at the Swinton match on Boxing Day was £5 2 0, of which one half was given to the Tom Williams Family Fund and the other to the Soldiers' and Sailors' Comforts Fund

---

leave from active service and announced the good news that popular winger George Callander had been heard from. This centrespread gives a whole list of players from which the teams were likely to be selected. It was often the case, during this difficult time, that line-ups were finally determined as the kick-off approached, depending on who had been able to turn up. Salford lost this particular match 5-0.

SALFORD FOOTBALL CLUB

Official Programme

(Issued by Authority of the Directors.)

No. 12   **February 5th, 1916.**   **Price 1d.**

The Dewsbury Match.

Commenting on the prospects of this match in our issue of January 22nd, we said "Given a decent day the game ought to be a sparkler." Well it was an excellent day and the game was in every way in keeping with the weather, and everyone present must have been delighted. Both teams played good, clean and honest football—not a semblance of foul play, all the players are entitled to thanks for their work. We were glad to annex the points but Mr. Wallwork's one slip nearly caused us to have to divide them, and his sigh of relief when the ball travelled wide could be heard a long way off.

It was a pity that owing to the late arrival of Dewsbury the game was limited to two 30's but the visitors are rather to be condoled with than blamed, as their train was due Manchester 2-10 and to make sure of a punctual start they ordered five taxis to meet them. But Football Committees propose and Railway Companies dispose—the train was forty minutes late.

The Wigan Match.

Once again has Central Park been fatal to us. We quite hoped to succeed last Saturday and in the early part of the game looked like doing so, but ultimately we had to give way and the final was 9. 3. against us. We used to look upon Central Park as a happy hunting ground—now we look upon it as, more or less, a cemetery.

Jack Bevon's Case.

We have received an acknowledgment from the County Committee of our protest against this player's suspension for an alleged offence in the Leigh match, and an expression of regret that nothing can be done as the Committee will not meet again before the suspension expires.

This is most unsatisfactory—the more that Bevon was suspended without an opportunity of defending himself. Bevon was ordered off on January 8th, and suspended three days later. No one expected the case would come up so early, indeed we did not know there was a meeting on Jan. 11th.

Benevolent Funds.

We are glad to say that the Williams' Family Fund is doing fairly well but we would like it to do "weller". Barrow have kindly promised to help by making a collection on their ground when we visit them on March 4th. We are very grateful to Barrow. We mentioned on January 8th that we intended to do something for the family of George Thom. We have arranged for the players of both sides to make a collection at half-time, the amount taken will be equally divided between the Thom fund and the Comforts Fund, which latter is much depleted. We are giving £5 from our Benevolent Fund to the Thom Fund and hope, later on, to play a benefit match or give half the gross gate of one of our ordinary fixtures.

Our Engagements.

To-day we meet Broughton Rangers whom we have already played twice this season. Let us hope for a good game and a good win.

Next Saturday Huddersfield will appear at the Willows. Their performances are so well known to every Rugby follower that we need not enlarge upon them. May the day be more propitious than the last one when Huddersfield were here.

The front cover of the programme for the match played against Broughton Rangers on 5 February 1916. It included news of a plan to raise money for the dependants of George Thom, a member of the club's 1914 championship side, who had passed away the previous December following injuries received in France. Salford won this try-less match 4-2.

Two Rugby League legends meet – Jimmy Lomas, nearing the end of a long career, and nineteen-year-old Jim Sullivan, destined for greatness. The occasion was the Salford versus Wigan encounter at The Willows on 10 March 1923, which ended scoreless. Lomas, after a long retirement, had surprisingly returned to Salford and played six matches during February and March of the 1922/23 season. Having been born in August 1879 (although some reports claim 1880 or 1882), he would have been in his forty-fourth year. This was the first season that the game was known as Rugby League, the Northern Rugby Football Union having voted to rename itself as the Rugby Football League during the summer of 1922.

2360 H. NORREY

The series of Pinnace cigarette cards, produced by Godfrey Phillips Ltd in 1923, have become much sought-after collectors' items. It contained an incredible total of 2,462 cards featuring players from Association Football, Rugby Union and Rugby League. Fourteen Salford players were included in the set, of which four are shown on this and the facing page. Harold (Harry) Norrey played on just 51 occasions for Salford between 1920 and 1925. Mostly operating as a wingman, he was the club's top try scorer in 1922/23 with 19 touchdowns.

E.C. (Teddy) Haines was a real stalwart of the team and played in 342 matches from 1921 until 1933. His loyalty to the club through the dark period of the 1920s was rewarded at the end of his career when the second row forward tasted success as a member of the victorious Lancashire Cup winning side of 1931. He represented England in 1927.

2350 E. HAINES

Walter Clegg's career at Salford began in 1913 and was to continue until 1927. He eventually established himself as the regular full-back after playing in several back positions in the earlier years. In total, he played 346 times for the Reds, although this included 78 wartime friendly games. His greatest moment, without doubt, was playing in the 1914 Championship final win over Huddersfield.

Centre three-quarter Chris Brockbank made only 35 appearances for the club during the 1922/23 season, preceded by 4 wartime friendly matches in 1918. It was after he retired as a player that the former Swinton back really made his reputation. Joining the back room staff at Huddersfield, he was to make two trips to Wembley, in 1933 and 1935, as the team's trainer and in 1950 he returned as the team manager of Warrington. He came away from the twin towers as a winner in 1933 and 1950.

F. SOUTHWARD,
SALFORD.

The Salford club's most famous player from the 1920s was Ferguson Southward, popularly known as Fergie. A Cumbrian born at Dearham, near Maryport, he joined Salford in 1921 and made 350 appearances before playing his final match in 1933. A graceful and quick centre, he scored 90 tries and 145 goals for the Reds. Like others who had remained loyal to the Salford cause during this low point in the club's fortunes, he was able to share in the glory of the 1931 Lancashire Cup final win over Swinton. He played for Cumberland 26 times from 1922 to 1932, which is easily the most appearances by a Salford player in county matches during the Northern Union and Rugby League period from 1896. This photograph is from the 1926/27 cigarette card series of fifty Famous Rugby Players produced by Imperial Tobacco.

On occasions, so-called 'silks', produced in full colour, were included in cigarette packets rather than picture cards. During the years of 1920, 1921 and 1922, BDV Cigarettes, manufactured by Godfrey Phillips Ltd, provided a series featuring twenty-seven Rugby League teams. The Salford drawing featured the famous red jersey, and the black socks that the team wore until the late 1920s.

LEAGUE COLOURS

SALFORD

B.D.V CIGARETTES

Four

Lance Todd and the Red Devils 1928-1940

The Salford supporters, who had stood by their team during the post-First World War period with very little to cheer, got their full reward as the 1930s approached. Lance Todd arrived on The Willows scene and, in just one season, he changed the club's fortunes around. The success he brought to Salford culminated in what is probably the greatest day in the history of the club, when victory was achieved at Wembley in the 1938 Rugby League Challenge Cup final. This is the victorious homecoming as the crowds pack Chapel Street to cheer their team as they make their way with the cup from Manchester's London Road (now Piccadilly) railway station to be received at Salford Town Hall.

Lance Todd took up his duties at Salford on 1 August 1928, having responded to a newspaper advertisement for a secretary/team manager. The New Zealander had arrived in 1907 as a member of the first ever Rugby League touring team to visit Great Britain. He was snapped up by Wigan in February 1908 and, after retiring as a player in 1914, had occupied his time as secretary to the North Shore Golf Club in Blackpool. Todd was an instant success, taking Salford from twenty-sixth in the league prior to his arrival, to fourth position in his first season. From then, until the outbreak of the Second World War in 1939, the 'Red Devils', as they would soon be famously known, dominated the British Rugby League scene. Today he is remembered through the annual award of the Lance Todd Trophy, presented to the player of the match in the Rugby League Challenge Cup final.

The first triumph under the Lance Todd influence was in 1931 when the Lancashire Challenge Cup was won in front of 26,471 at The Cliff ground, the home of Broughton Rangers. The victims were local rivals Swinton, with Salford winning 10-8. It was the first trophy collected by the club since the 1914 championship win, as this newspaper cartoonist eagerly points out. The victory made up for an earlier defeat in the 1929 Lancashire Cup final.

The official team photograph of the side that clinched the Lancashire Cup for Salford in 1931. From left to right, back row: Fred Shaw, Teddy Haines, Barney Hudson, Jack Feetham. Third row: Gus Risman, Emlyn Jenkins, Fergie Southward, Sammy Miller, Joe Bradbury. Second row (seated): Lance B. Todd (secretary/manager), Billy Williams (captain), C.B. Riley (chairman), Alf Middleton, Tom Coates (trainer). Front row (on floor): Billy Watkins, Reg Meek. For players like Haines, Southward and Meek, it was a moment to savour after the dark days of just a few seasons previous.

SALFORD CHAMPIONS OF THE
RUGBY LEAGUE

Billy Williams, the Salford captain, with the championship cup after the presentation by Mr. Haworth, chairman of the Rugby League. Bryn Evans, Swinton's captain, is also in the picture.

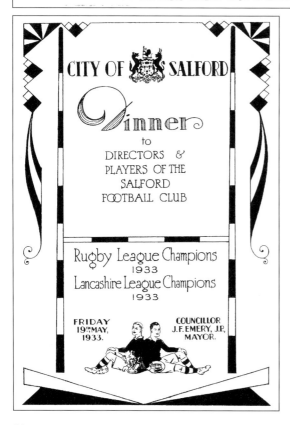

Salford quickly became the dominant force in the game in Britain and the championship was recaptured after almost twenty years when Swinton were beaten by 15-5 in the 1932/33 final at Wigan. The crowd numbered 18,000. This newspaper photograph captures the moment of triumph for team captain Billy Williams as he receives the magnificent trophy.

Civic receptions given by the City of Salford to the players and officials of the club became regular events during the 1930s. This one was at the Salford Town Hall where the Salford club were entertained by the mayor, J.F. Emery. It was held to honour the club in capturing the 1932/33 Northern Rugby League Championship and Lancashire League Championship titles. The official menu card contained the programme of events, including the official toasts, the dinner menu itself and, of course, the wine list!

The Salford team in 1933/34. From left to right, back row: Bert Day, Harold Osbaldestin, Barney Hudson, Aubrey Casewell, Alf Middleton, Paddy Dalton, Jack Feetham, Joe Bradbury, Cliff Evans. Middle row (seated): Gus Risman, C.B. Riley (chairman), Billy Williams (captain), Lance B. Todd (secretary/manager), Bob Brown. Front row: Emlyn Jenkins (kneeling), Les Pearson, Sammy Miller, Billy Watkins (kneeling). The 1933/34 season would finish with Salford suffering their only championship final defeat of the decade, losing to Wigan at Warrington by 15-3 in front of 31,564 spectators. Nonetheless, three trophies were still on display in this picture (from left to right): Salford Royal Hospitals Cup, Lancashire League Championship Trophy, Leeds Sevens Trophy. The latter was won at Headingley in May 1933 after defeating Keighley in the final. The Hospitals Cup was an annual charity contest that also involved Broughton Rangers and Swinton.

The 1933/34 season was a personal milestone for Wigan-born winger Bob Brown. His total of 45 tries eclipsed the twenty-seven-year-old record set by Jimmy Lomas. In the process he also established a record try-scoring run of nine consecutive matches, equalled in May 1996 by Nathan McAvoy. Signed in 1932, Brown was a regular member of the side throughout the 1930s and shared in the club's 1938 Wembley glory. Although he did not gain international recognition, he was selected for Lancashire on 9 occasions.

Saturday, Octdber 21st, 1933.

KICK-OFF   -   **3-0** P.M.

SALFORD.

1—Qasaldestin

2—Brown   3—Miller   4—Risman   5—Pearson or Dobing

6—Watkins   7—Evans

8—Williams (Capt.)   9—Day   10—Bradbury

11—Casewell   12—Middleton or Dalton

13—Feetham

12—Rugg

10—O'Connor   6—Gibbs

9—Madsen   8—Little   2—Curran

15—Doonar   17—Gilbert

25—Ridley   14—Brown   23—Hey   24—Pearce

19—McMillan (Capt.)

AUSTRALIA.

Referee - Mr. J. E. TAYLOR.

Linesmen - Messrs. W. WOOLAM & J. ATKINSON.

BETTER-UN VETERAN - - *By Gannon*

The team sheet for the match against the 1933 Australian tourists on 21 October. A crowd of 15,761 watched Salford secure a famous victory by 16-9. This followed four failures against previous Australian touring sides. The Reds repeated the feat against the 1937 Australians by 11-8. Salford have only won this fixture twice.

A contemporary cartoon by Gannon describing the Salford victory over the 1933 Australian touring side. Former hero Jimmy Lomas, who was at the match as a spectator, even gets a mention. Harry Sunderland, a journalist, broadcaster and manager of the Australian touring team, is also featured. Sunderland was later the prime mover in instigating the Lance Todd Trophy.

Jean Galia organised and led a short pioneering tour of England, under Rugby League rules, by a 'France' team in 1934. This was a consequence of a dispute over alleged professionalism in French Rugby Union, which resulted in France being excluded from the Five Nations tournament from 1931 to 1947. Galia's team visited Salford on 26 March where they were beaten 34-13 in front of 7,000 curious fans. Paddy Dalton, the Salford forward, played for the visitors in their three-quarter line, due to a shortage of players through injuries in earlier games. Overall, the tour was a success and sowed the first seed for the birth of the French Rugby League. Here, the popular cartoonist, Nix, captures the action from this historic match with a good portion of humour thrown in.

SALFORD RUGBY FOOTBALL CLUB

PROGRAMME

OF

Visit to PARIS, LYONS, BEZIERS, ALBI, PERPIGNAN and VILLENEUVE-SUR-LOT.

———

SATURDAY, OCTOBER 20th

to

TUESDAY, NOVEMBER 6th, 1934.

———

THOS. COOK & SON, LTD.,
Head Office : BERKELEY STREET, LONDON, W.1.

———

WAGONS-LITS/COOK,
World Travel Service
PARIS : 2, Place de la Madeleine.
LYONS : 105, Rue de l'Hotel de Ville.

(1507/10/31 8.)

Salford became the first of several English club sides to visit France on a propaganda tour, following an initial trip by a Yorkshire Select party containing mostly Leeds players in May 1934. Wagon-Lites organised Salford's visit and provided a full itinerary for each member of the party. Salford travelled overnight to France immediately after winning the 1934 Lancashire Cup final against Wigan and went into action in the first of their six matches the next day.

The team line-ups taken from the 'programme officiel' for the third match of the Salford tour of France against Beziers on 28 October, which was won 41-8. Warrington referee Holbrook, who covered all the tour games, travelled with Salford as an official member of the tour party.

The Salford players join their hosts XIII Catalan before the penultimate match of their tour, played in Perpignan on 2 November. Salford won 41-16 and went on to complete a clean sweep, winning all six games.

54

The card from the official reception given by Mayor E.A. Hardy at Salford Town Hall to celebrate winning the 1934 Lancashire Cup. Jim Sullivan, whose Wigan team had lost that final 21-12 in front of 35,544 fans at Swinton, was a guest of honour. The reception was delayed until November, due to the club's French tour. The guest list extended to everyone who had been in the party to France including referee Holbrook and Harry Sunderland, who worked as a journalist on the trip. Salford's style of fast, open rugby had won them many admirers in France. It earned the name 'Les Diables Rouges', the famous 'Red Devils' title that has been associated with the team ever since. Unlike other official dinners, this menu was not printed in French! As it said inside the card: 'It is considered that owing to the surfeit of French dishes the tourists will have faced in France, this menu in English will be appreciated.'

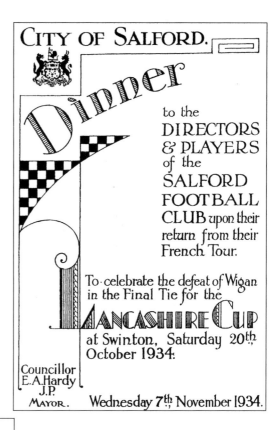

CITY OF SALFORD.

Dinner

to the DIRECTORS & PLAYERS of the SALFORD FOOTBALL CLUB upon their return from their French Tour.

To·celebrate the defeat of Wigan in the Final Tie for the LANCASHIRE CUP at Swinton, Saturday 20th October 1934.

Councillor E.A.Hardy J.P. MAYOR.

Wednesday 7th November 1934.

Salford Football Club Company (1914) Ltd.

TWENTY-FIRST

ANNUAL REPORT

to be Submitted at a

GENERAL MEETING OF THE COMPANY,

to be held at the

REGISTERED OFFICES OF THE COMPANY, WILLOWS ROAD, WEASTE,

On Friday, 12th July, 1935, at 8 p.m.

Your Directors beg to submit the Accounts for the year ending May 31st, 1935.

Once more they are pleased to report a successful season. The First team won the Lancashire Cup for the second time and for the third consecutive season won the Lancashire League Championship Cup. Fourth place in the Northern Rugby League table was attained, the team being beaten in the Semi-final for the League Championship.

Following the Lancashire Cup final a short tour of France was made in which Six matches were played all of which were won by substantial margins, and very valuable propaganda work was done in that country.

A. J. Risman again kicked more than 100 goals during the season this being the third consecutive season he has accomplished this feat.

An extraordinary season of injuries and illness severely handicapped the Club for a long period but it is hoped that the Summer will have restored the players concerned to their accustomed fitness and the coming season is looked forward to with confidence. All of last season's players are expected to be available and in addition every effort will be made to strengthen the team as opportunity occurs.

The building of a new covered stand on the popular side is being proceeded with and increased comfort and convenience for the spectators is being aimed at.

The Co-operation of the Supporters' Association has again proved invaluable and the continued good work by them is a great asset to the Club.

Messrs. J. Priestley, F. Mattinson, T. A. Rich and F. H. Wellwood, Directors, retire and being eligible offer themselves for re-election.

By Order of the Board,

C. B. RILEY, Chairman.

The annual report from club chairman, C.B. Riley, for season 1934/35. One of the interesting items in the balance sheet that accompanied the report was a reference to the Baseball Account. The prophetically titled Salford Reds baseball team played during the summer months on Saturday evenings. The core of the team was made up from the club's rugby players, such as Gus Risman, Sammy Miller and Dave Schofield. They played their first ever match on 25 May 1935 against the Oldham Greyhounds, who won by 9 runs to 8, at The Willows in front of a 4,000 crowd. The 'home base' was situated at the Willows Road/Kennedy Road corner of the rugby field.

Salford's representatives in the 1936 tour team to Australia and New Zealand on board ship. All five had played in the decisive third Test match with Australia at Sydney Cricket Ground on 12 June. Under Gus Risman's captaincy, 53,546 witnessed Great Britain's 12-7 victory to retain the Ashes trophy. From left to right, back: Barney Hudson, Allan Edwards. Front row: Billy Watkins, Risman, Emlyn Jenkins. Hudson, from County Durham, was the lone Englishman amongst four Welsh colleagues.

The tourists returned to action in mid-September and shared in the team's 1936 Lancashire Cup final win over Wigan by 5-2 on 17 October. The match is depicted here by the newspaper cartoonist, Ray. It was Salford's fourth success in the competition and the third consecutive year that they had beaten Wigan in the final, following up a 15-7 win in 1935.

The 1936/37 Salford team display their silverware. From left to right, back row: Barney Hudson, Bert Cambridge, Bert Day. Third row: George Harris, Joe Bradbury, Paddy Dalton, Jack Feetham, Harold Osbaldestin. Second row: Allan Edwards, C.B. Riley (chairman), Albert Gear, Gus Risman (captain), Billy Williams, Lance Todd (secretary/manager), Emlyn Jenkins. Front row: Billy Watkins, Sammy Miller. Salford took the Rugby League Championship title for the third time, beating Warrington 13-11 at Wigan, watched by 31,500. The trophies on display are, from left to right: Lancashire League Championship Trophy, Rugby League Championship Trophy, Lancashire Challenge Cup.

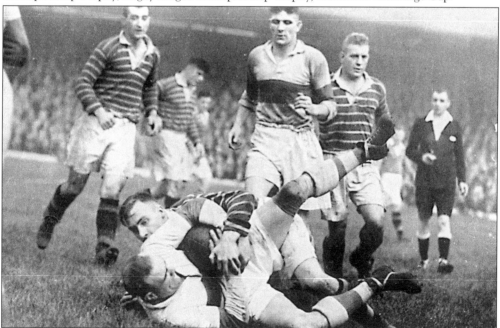

Salford (with band on white jersey) against Huddersfield on 3 October 1937 at The Willows. Paddy Dalton supports as bustling winger Barney Hudson is tackled close to the touchline. Salford won this League Championship encounter 38-8, but finished the season sixth, the lowest placing since 1931.

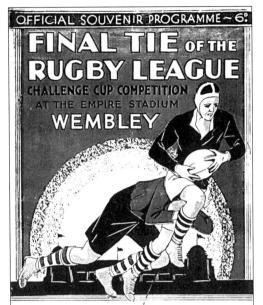

FINAL TIE OF THE
RUGBY LEAGUE
CHALLENGE CUP COMPETITION
AT THE EMPIRE STADIUM
WEMBLEY

SATURDAY, MAY 7, 1938

BARROW
v.
SALFORD

KICK-OFF 3.30 P.M.

In 1938 Salford finally achieved what, for them, had become the holy grail, when Barrow were beaten in the Rugby League Challenge Cup final at Wembley. It is the only time, to date, that Salford have managed to get their hands on the most prized of all of Rugby League's trophies.

The Salford players line up to be introduced to Donald Bradman, the Australian cricket star, who was destined to receive a knighthood. One of the greatest batsmen of all time, Bradman was in England as the captain of the Australian touring team. Gus Risman introduces his team in the traditional pre-match presentation. The players are, from left to right: Billy Williams, Bert Day, Paddy Dalton (shaking hands), Dai Davies, Harold Thomas, Albert Gear and Billy Watkins.

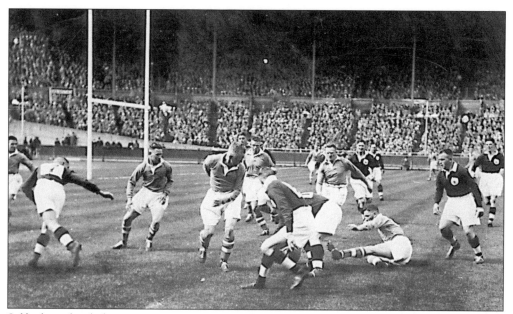

Salford, in the darker jerseys, put pressure on the Barrow line at Wembley. Harold Osbaldestin (slightly obscured by Allan Edwards) looks set to bring the ball back into play. Other Salford players are Billy Watkins (7) on the left, who appears to have overrun the play, and Bob Brown on the right. Salford played in their traditional red jerseys and Barrow in royal blue.

Gus Risman is held up by Barrow prop Bill Skelly. Harold Thomas, looking on, pleads for a pass inside which, apparently, did not arrive on this occasion.

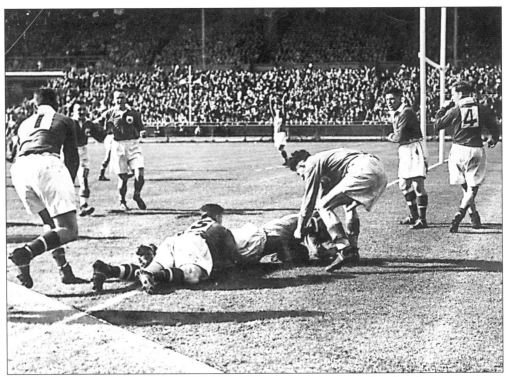

At 4-4 and with a few minutes remaining, the cup final appeared to be heading for a replay at Wigan. Then, in the 79th minute, young centre Albert Gear created the moment of glory when he followed up his own kick ahead, near the Barrow line, to score the winning try.

Gus Risman attempts to convert Albert Gear's late match winner by adding on the extra two goal points. The kick was not successful, sailing wide of the posts as the final whistle sounded and Salford finished victors by 7-4.

Salford captain Gus Risman leaves the Royal Box in triumph after receiving the Challenge Cup from Donald Bradman. Risman was to repeat the feat in 1952 as captain and coach of Workington Town. The other Salford players are Harold Thomas, Bob Brown and Bert Day.

The official team photograph to commemorate the 1938 Rugby League Challenge Cup success. From left to right, back row: Jack Feetham, Dai Davies, Harold Thomas, Bob Brown, Joe Bradbury. Third row (standing): Allan Edwards, Paddy Dalton, Harold Osbaldestin, Billy Williams, Barney Hudson, Bert Day, Albert Gear. Second row (seated): Lance B. Todd (secretary/manager), C.B. Riley (chairman), Gus Risman (captain), J.B. Goldstraw (vice-chairman), Jack Dawson (trainer). Front row (on floor): Sammy Miller, Billy Watkins.

THE EMPIRE STADIUM WEMBLEY

FINAL TIE
OF THE
RUGBY LEAGUE
CHALLENGE CUP
COMPETITION

SALFORD

HALIFAX

SATURDAY, MAY 6, 1939
KICK-OFF 3.30 P.M.
OFFICIAL PROGRAMME SIXPENCE

Salford returned to Wembley in 1939 and must have fancied their chances of retaining the trophy. However, the combination of a 'flu bug, which hit the team in the week leading up to the final, and a powerful Halifax performance on the day was decisive.

Halifax centre Jack Treen crosses the Salford try line at Wembley for his team's second touchdown of the opening half-hour. The Yorkshire side took the cup with a convincing 20-3 victory.

The 1939 Championship final, played at Manchester City's Maine Road ground, drew a Rugby League record crowd, for the time, of 69,504. As at Wembley in 1938, Salford secured a dramatic, late victory. With seven minutes remaining, wingman Allan Edwards followed up Albert Gear's kick to touch down, snatching the lead and victory from Castleford's grasp.

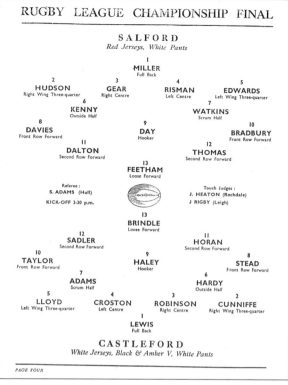

RUGBY LEAGUE CHAMPIONSHIP FINAL

SALFORD
Red Jerseys, White Pants

1
MILLER
Full Back

2   3   4   5
HUDSON   **GEAR**   **RISMAN**   **EDWARDS**
Right Wing Three-quarter   Right Centre   Left Centre   Left Wing Three-quarter

6   7
KENNY   **WATKINS**
Outside Half   Scrum Half

8   9   10
DAVIES   **DAY**   **BRADBURY**
Front Row Forward   Hooker   Front Row Forward

11   12
DALTON   **THOMAS**
Second Row Forward   Second Row Forward

13
FEETHAM
Loose Forward

Referee :   Touch Judges :
S. ADAMS (Hull)   J. HEATON (Rochdale)
KICK-OFF 3-30 p.m.   J RIGBY (Leigh)

13
BRINDLE
Loose Forward

12   11
SADLER   **HORAN**
Second Row Forward   Second Row Forward

10   9   8
TAYLOR   **HALEY**   **STEAD**
Front Row Forward   Hooker   Front Row Forward

7   6
ADAMS   **HARDY**
Scrum Half   Outside Half

5   4   3   2
LLOYD   **CROSTON**   **ROBINSON**   **CUNNIFFE**
Left Wing Three-quarter   Left Centre   Right Centre   Right Wing Three-quarter

1
LEWIS
Full Back

CASTLEFORD
White Jerseys, Black & Amber V, White Pants

Young Welsh prop Dai Davies (left), and skipper Gus Risman proudly show off the Rugby League Championship trophy, having beaten Castleford 8-6 in a pulsating final. It was to be Salford's last big triumph for over thirty years. Nobody could have realised at the time, but the Second World War was just four months away and Salford's great side would break up as a consequence.

B. (BARNEY) HUDSON, SALFORD

Bernard Hudson, known throughout the game as 'Barney', became one of the great personalities of the club following his signing from Hartlepool Rovers Rugby Union Club in 1928. He went on to make 421 appearances for Salford and his 282 career tries remained a club record until surpassed by Maurice Richards nearly forty years later. A big man, he was just as likely to run through his opponents as around them. He toured down under twice, represented Great Britain on 8 occasions and England on 6. He retired as a player in 1946 and later joined the coaching staff at Salford. This picture is taken from a series of cards that appeared in Senior Service cigarette packets in 1935. The series, titled 'Sporting Events and Stars', contained 96 cards and featured several of Salford's heroes of that time. They were produced by J.A. Pattreiouex of Manchester.

Jack Feetham was one of the few 'ready-made' Rugby League stars signed by Lance Todd. Already an international player, he transferred from Hull Kingston Rovers in 1929 and became a key member of the Salford pack through the ten successful years that followed. A fearsome loose forward, he provided great cover for his half-backs. A tourist in 1932, he gained 8 caps for Great Britain and represented Yorkshire 9 times. He appeared in 409 matches for the Red Devils and his 109 tries created a club record for a forward until Mike Coulman passed it in 1980. His 21 tries in 1931/32 is still the most by a Salford forward in one season. This picture card of Feetham was printed in colour and was part of a set of fifty called, predictably, 'Football Caricatures'. They were issued in 1935 and produced by Hignett Brothers and Company of Liverpool.

HIGNETT'S CIGARETTES

J. FEETHAM (SALFORD)

Augustus John Ferdinand (Gus) Risman is considered by many to be the greatest player ever to wear the famous red jersey of Salford. This view is certainly endorsed by the fact that he was one of the original eight inductees into the Rugby League Hall of Fame in October 1988. Born in Cardiff, he was signed in 1929 when he was just seventeen years old and played 427 times for the club. He was the complete player: fast, skilful, strong in defence, a master tactician and a great leader. Although he played his final match for Salford in 1946, his playing career continued until 1954, reputed to be the longest time span ever by a professional Rugby League player. His career total of 873 matches is second only to Wigan's Jim Sullivan. For Salford, he scored 2,007 points from 143 tries and 789 goals. He set a club record for goals (116) and points (277) in 1933/34, which was finally broken by David Watkins in 1970/71. He toured Australia and New Zealand three times and was the tour captain on the final occasion, in 1946. On his return, he signed for the fledgling Workington Town as their player-coach and took them to both championship and Wembley success in just six seasons.

Broughton Rangers v. Salford

Saturday, 18th May, 1940   Kick-off 3-30

BROUGHTON RANGERS

Colours : Blue & White Quarters, White Pants

Right Wing   Left Wing

1
Rees

2   3   4   5
Jenkins, T.   Walker   Green   Jenkins, G.

6   7
Bulcock   Smith

8   9   10   11   12   13
Lee   Jones   Manning   Cattlin   Spruce   Brown

Referee :   Touch Judges :
G. S. Phillips,   H. W. Bateman.
Widnes.   H. Ainsworth.

Feetham   Thomas   Dalton   Gardner   Jones   Davies
15   12   11   10   9

Watkins   Harrison
7   6

Edwards   Risman   Williams   Hudson or Miller
5   4   3   2

Miller
1

Left Wing   Right Wing

SALFORD

Colours : Red Shirts and White Pants

Should any Alteration be made a Notice Board will be sent round giving the Player's Name and Number

NO MATCH for
ELECTRICITY
JUST SWITCH ON

VISIT THE
ELECTRICITY SHOWROOM
23, Tiviot Dale, Stockport
STO 4631

NOTES AND COMMENTS

Regarding the Summer Cup Competition we have now played two matches, with Leigh last Saturday, which was won, and with Salford at Salford on Monday last, when victory went to Salford.

It was regretable the match last Saturday resulted in two unfortunate accidents to players—(so as not to be misunderstood let me state here that both these mishaps were the result of pure accidents)—Thompson, the Rangers' captain, sustained a foot injury which necessitated the Doctor putting a splint under the foot ; then the accident to Ord, the Leigh player, who sustained a broken nose, again called upon the Doctor for his attention.

To Dr. Wilson, of the Stockport County Club, we tender our sincere and grateful thanks for all his help and kindness in the manner in which he attended to these players.

Although the match was very poorly attended the game was keenly contested, with the Rangers deserving of their win.

On Monday, at Salford, the Rangers gave a much improved display, and welcomed back to the team two of their players (Smith and Walker) who have hitherto not been able to play for the team this season, on account of being unable to get away from work, but we are pleased to say that we are hoping

that the arrangements now made, will enable them to play in the remaining matches. Considering it was their first appearance both played well and helped in the general improvement of the team's play.

As was expected, with the coming of the serious turn of events in the War over the week-end, we had to do without the services of our Soldier players, who were unable to obtain leave, and so far as this season is concerned we may have seen the last of them ; if this be the case, we send them our greetings, and in wishing them good luck, hope that we may all soon be re-united and with things back to normal, fighting it out on the football field once again. Good luck Boys, and a speedy return.

Congratulations to Swinton who are now the champions of the Lancashire Section of the War-time League, and who will now meet Bradford, the champions of the Yorkshire Section, in the first leg of the " Championship of the Rugby League," at Swinton to-day, the return match being played at Bradford on Saturday next.

We wish them the best of luck and hope that they will prove the victors and bring the " Championship " to Lancashire. If this be the case, it should bring the crowd to see them when we meet Swinton in the Summer Cup Competition on Wednesday evening, 12th June, at Edgeley Park, kick-off 7 p.m.

After war was declared, the 1939/40 season was replaced by more manageable county leagues. In May 1940, this was followed with an experimental Summer Cup competition. Salford's second match was away to Broughton Rangers at Stockport County football ground as Rangers' own ground had been requisitioned for the war effort. After beating Broughton 13-0 at home a few days earlier, the 65-15 Salford win was larger than expected. Gus Risman equalled his 1933 club record of 13 goals in a match. Clubs were already struggling to put teams on the field and 'due to financial difficulties' Salford ceased playing in December 1940. They would not resume until August 1945.

The souvenir programme from a cabaret evening held in honour of Salford's success at Wembley in 1938. Described on the cover as a 'party', the main event was the presentation to the club of a replica of the Rugby League Challenge Cup by hosts Groves and Whitnall. The local brewery was actually Salford's landlord up to 1933 and retained close links with the club. The presentation evening was staged at the Cattle Market Hotel in Cross Lane on 12 October 1938. Naturally, this was one of Groves and Whitnall's many establishments in the area at that time. From 1954 the trophy was competed for under the name of the Red Rose Cup as an annual pre-season charity match against Swinton.

The programme for a testimonial match given in Lance Todd's honour and autographed by the great man. Staged in September 1938, it acknowledged his ten years of wonderful service to the club. It is some measure of the warmth felt by the fans towards him that the idea for such a match, usually reserved for players, came from the Salford Supporters' Association. In the programme notes, Todd singled out the club's win at Wembley in 1938 as his greatest moment. 'It was the culmination of years of hard work and the realisation of the dream of everybody connected with the club' he said. When the Second World War started, Todd joined the Home Guard. Tragically, he was killed in a road accident in November 1942. It was the end of a wonderful era for Salford.

SALFORD FOOTBALL CLUB CO. LTD. 1601

Souvenir Programme

L. B. Todd's Testimonial

SALFORD v. LEEDS

Tuesday, Sept. 6th, 1938

Kick-off 6-45.

ONE PENNY

Five
Post-War Depression
1945-1964

The end of the Second World War signalled a boom in sporting attendance figures, as the nation sought entertainment and relaxation after years of turmoil, and Rugby League was no exception. The first home match of the second post-war season, 1946/47, saw Salford entertain Warrington in a Lancashire cup-tie. In this picture, a packed Willows crowd of 13,431 watches as Salford winger Harry Dagnan races for the try-line with the Warrington cover defence desperately trying to halt his progress. Despite the large attendances, good times were disappearing at Salford. Lance Todd had gone and what remained of his great players were now at the veteran stage in sporting terms. The next twenty years would get progressively worse and, by the 1960s, the club would be praying for another miracle as results hit their lowest ebb since the '20s.

Reg Jones of Salford, playing at stand-off half, brings down his Warrington namesake Les Jones in the Lancashire Cup. This was a first round tie played at The Willows on 7 September 1946, which Salford won 10-3.

More action from the Lancashire Cup clash as Salford second row forward Jack Brown gets to grips with Warrington second rower Taylor.

Dai Moses appears to score a try for Salford in a match at Belle Vue Rangers in 1946, but has just put a foot into touch. The Rangers, previously known as Broughton Rangers, transferred from their former base at The Cliff to the Belle Vue Stadium in 1933, but did not adopt their new title until the 1946/47 season. Note the speedway track of the famous Belle Vue Aces around the outside of the playing area.

Salford forward Jack Brown attempts an unorthodox overhead pass in the match at Belle Vue. He had just received a back pass from a colleague who appears to be still receiving attention from an opponent. The scoreboard in the background indicates that Salford are 8-0 down at this stage and they eventually lost 13-5 in front of a 15,000 crowd. The match was played on 28 September 1946 and was the second of a barren spell that would bring 17 defeats in 18 games. Brown moved to Huddersfield in November 1951.

George Curran in his Great Britain jersey. A versatile forward who could play in any pack position, including hooker, he was one of the few bright spots for Salford fans in the early post-war years. Having been signed before the Second World War had broken out, he waited until 1945/46 for his first full season. His 20 appearances for Salford during that campaign clearly impressed and he was selected to join his club captain Gus Risman on the 1946 tour to Australasia. His 12 matches for England, whilst at Salford, is a record for the club. After 175 appearances in Salford colours, he transferred to Wigan in 1950 and then moved on to Huddersfield at the end of 1951. He enjoyed Wembley success with both of those teams: Wigan in 1951 and Huddersfield in 1953 (the latter success being shared with his ex-Salford colleague Jack Brown).

Salford three-quarter Taylor, a recent capture from the famous Warrington amateur club, Rylands Recs, evades the Halifax defence as he kicks ahead. Halifax eventually won 23-0. Played on 5 October 1946, this match was Salford's biggest defeat at The Willows since January 1925.

More packed terraces at The Willows to see the visit of St Helens on 19 October 1946. Salford wingman Harry Dagnan passes to the supporting George Curran on the halfway line. In this move, Curran went on a barnstorming run which was finally halted on the Saints' twenty-five-yard line. Once again Salford were beaten at home, this time by 11-2.

Salford take on the Challenge Cup holders Wakefield Trinity on 15 February 1947. George Curran is tackled close to the Trinity try-line. The match finished as a scoreless draw. Note the snow on the edge of The Willows pitch.

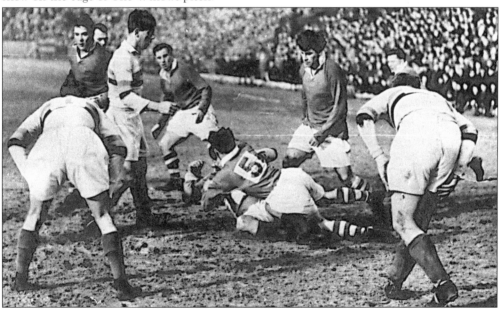

Salford's wing three-quarter, Syd Williams (5), is brought down just five yards short of the Bradford Northern try-line. This was a first round, second leg, Rugby League Challenge Cup match played at Odsal Stadium on 12 March 1947. In the early post-war years, up to 1953/54, the opening rounds were staged over two legs. This was fortunate for Bradford, who had already lost the first leg at Salford 5-2, but took the tie thanks to a 10-0 win in this match. They went on to make their Wembley debut in the first of three successive cup finals at the stadium, becoming the first club to achieve this feat.

George Curran (13) scoring Salford's second try against Barrow on his way to a personal hat-trick, as the Reds won 21-5. The match, played in a blizzard at The Willows, took place on 21 February 1948.

The first home match of the 1950/51 season against Huddersfield on 26 August. Grounded centre three-quarter Jack Davies, who normally played at stand-off half, appears to have failed in his attempted pass to the supporting Frank Alder (10). Huddersfield won this encounter 28-5. This was an early season blow to the Red Devils, who were hoping to build on their fifth placing of the previous season. However, Salford slid down the table to finish nineteenth and were not to breach the top ten again until 1967/68.

Salford, 1951/52. From left to right, back row: Dignum, D. Davies, McKinney, Kenny, Rogers, Grainger. Middle row: Hartley, J. Davies, Harrison (captain), Danby, Williams. Front row: Hesketh, Hindle. Prop forward Dai Davies and scrum-half Tommy Harrison were survivors from Lance Todd's great 1930s team. Davies, in his last full season, played 370 times for Salford and Harrison, who retired in 1955, made 359 appearances. Tom Danby, an England RU international, was in the 1950 Rugby League party to Australasia. Tom McKinney, signed from Scottish RU despite his Irish ancestry, was chosen for the 1954 tour. This picture was taken on 27 October 1951 before a 19-5 home loss against Oldham.

Salford 1952/53. From left to right, back row: Peter Marston, Jack Rogers, Frank Alder, Tom Danby, Fred Smith, Frank Birkin, Brian Keavney. Front row: Fred Halton, Dai Moses, Alan Easterbrook, Tom McKinney, Bryn Hartley, Jack Davies. Classy stand-off Jack Davies was a former Welsh Rugby Union international and became a consistent scorer for the Red Devils. He registered 49 tries and 469 goals in his 241 appearances and was the top goal and point scorer in each of his eight seasons at the club from 1947 until 1955. This picture was taken at Salford on 26 December 1952, at the second of three matches played over Christmas on consecutive days. Widnes were beaten 8-0.

DAI MOSES
Salford R.F.C.

The News Chronicle & Daily Despatch, a morning newspaper that used to appear in the Manchester area at the time, issued a series of player 'Pocket Portrait' cards in January 1956 that featured several Rugby League clubs. Thirteen Salford players were in the set, including the four shown on this and the facing page. Dai Moses had a long association with Salford. Initially signed from Welsh Rugby Union in 1945, he made 328 appearances before joining rivals Swinton in 1958 following a dispute with Gus Risman, who was the Salford coach at that time. Remembered as an uncompromising prop forward, he began his career in the back row and became an integral part of Swinton's return to power in the late 1950s. He came back to The Willows in 1970 to join the coaching staff and added the role of head groundsman to his CV in the mid-1970s.

JOHN CHESHIRE
Salford R.F.C.

John Cheshire was yet another in the long list of signings from Welsh Rugby Union. A strong centre three-quarter, he was particularly renowned for his defensive qualities. Signed in 1955 from the Cross Keys club, he made 255 appearances over eight seasons before transferring to Oldham in 1963. During the second half of his time at Salford he took over the goal-kicking duties and landed 141 to add to his contribution of 43 tries. In fact, Cheshire did not consider himself a marksman but took on the job in the absence of a recognised kicker at the club during this period.

Harry Council was a hard and straight-running back row and, latterly, prop forward, who was signed in 1955 from the Dukinfield Rugby Union club. His eleven seasons at Salford, which were plagued by injuries towards the end, covered 262 appearances. He was to return to the limelight, along with Moses and Cheshire, when the three of them were invited to the special pre-match presentation to Salford's centenary match in 1979.

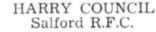

HARRY COUNCIL
Salford R.F.C.

GRAHAM JONES
Salford R.F.C.

Graham Jones was signed from the Penarth Rugby Union club in 1954, originally to play as a stand-off half. After three years, however, it was felt that his exceptional pace and side-stepping technique would make him an ideal wingman. He was an instant success in this new role and, in the 1959/60 season, he recorded 27 touchdowns. This equalled George Aspinall's post-war record in 1947/48 and was not overtaken until fellow Welshman, Maurice Richards, scored 35 in 1971/72. Jones registered 119 tries for Salford from 239 appearances.

Salford, playing in white jerseys with a red band, in action at Swinton's former Station Road ground on Easter Saturday, 17 April 1954. Salford scrum-half Tommy Harrison attempts to tackle Rees Thomas whilst his half-back partner, Jack Davies, moves in to cover. Salford won the match 13-2.

Salford 1956/57. From left to right, back row: Eric Ayles, Jim Parr, Frank Alder, Frank Boardman, Hugh Duffy, Derek Fieldhouse, Ron Walker. Front row: Fred Smith, Frank Dodd, Graham Jones, Brian Keavney, Brian Hanley, John Cheshire. Former Scotland Rugby Union international Duffy was signed from Jed-Forest in 1955. Recognised as one of the best loose forwards in the game at the time, he played 241 times for Salford before joining Halifax in 1962. This team picture was taken on 11 September 1956 before the Lancashire Cup second round match against Oldham at Salford. Oldham won 31-0.

On Guy Fawkes Night in 1958, Salford literally broke new ground by entertaining Leeds in a 'home' match staged at Old Trafford. The original fixture, scheduled for 28 October, had been postponed as Leeds had been otherwise engaged in winning the Yorkshire Cup final against Wakefield Trinity. Salford chairman George Cadman expresses his thanks to Manchester United in the programme notes. The perfect result did not happen for Salford, however, and Leeds won 22-17 in front of 8,373 fans.

Salford centre Bob Preece evades Ken Irvine's clutches to touch down against the 1959 Australian tourists, giving Salford a dramatic 17-12 lead with only 15 minutes remaining; Graham Jones is the supporting Salford player. Salford eventually lost this thriller 22-20. Note the spectators sat inside the perimeter fence, something that would be banned today for safety reasonss. The match was played on 26 September and the attendance was 11,088.

SALFORD
versus
LEEDS

WEDNESDAY, NOVEMBER 5th, 1958.   *Kick-off* 7-30 p.m.

THANK YOU, MANCHESTER UNITED !

Salford Directors' appreciation of a magnanimous and sporting gesture.

I cannot let the opportunity pass of expressing through the medium of this programme how appreciative I and my fellow directors are of Manchester United's magnanimous and sporting gesture in permitting us to play our postponed match with Leeds at their superbly equipped Old Trafford ground and I wish to thank Mr. H. P. Hardman, their chairman, and his colleagues for their most kindly act, the like of which I have never known in my long association with various kinds of sport.

When I made the suggestion to Mr. Hardman, the acceptance of the idea was spontaneous—no discussion on this or that, but an outstretched hand to assist us to avoid a financial loss on one of our best fixtures which had to be postponed on account of Leeds being engaged in the Yorkshire Cup Final.

Manchester United, who have a reputation second to none throughout the world of sport, have revealed to us another side of their character which I am sure will not have passed unnoticed by the public at large.

Again I say, *Thank you, Manchester United !*

GEORGE S. CADMAN,
(Chairman, Salford R.L.F.C.)

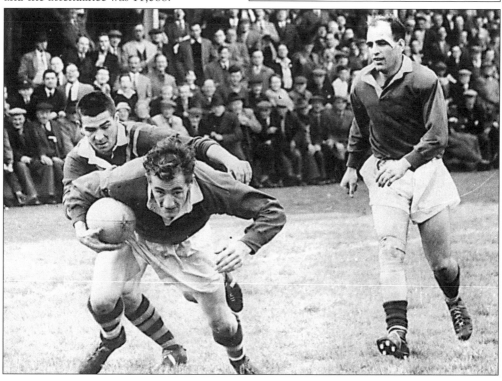

A murky winter's Saturday afternoon at The Willows as Salford look to clear their line against Widnes at the Cricket Ground end. Arthur Gregory (on left) has just played the ball backwards to Frank Alder (picking up). The other players, all representing Salford are, from the left: Jack Brennan, Harry Council, Billy Banks, Frank Boardman, George Parsons, Bryn Hartley and Hugh Duffy. Note the former club pavilion in the background. This match was played on 12 December 1959 and won 23-6 by Salford.

Salford at home to Rochdale Hornets on 2 April 1960. Loose forward Hugh Duffy (light jersey) halts Rochdale attack as Cumbrian three-quarter Syd Lowden prepares to lend a hand. Salford won this match 13-6. The light coloured jersey, worn by Salford as an alternative strip, was actually pale blue, although it looks white in the monochrome photograph.

The once traditional Easter Saturday derby fixture against Swinton at The Willows on 16 April 1960. Swinton's international full-back Ken Gowers attempts to score by diving over his opposite number, Arthur Gregory. Salford back row forward Roy Stott (on right) rushes across to help out his defence. Swinton, who were a power in the sport at the time, won 25-5.

The Salford team at Swinton on 12 August 1961, prior to the annual pre-season charity match for the Red Rose Cup. From left to right, back row: Harry Council, John Cheshire, Hugh Duffy, Bryn Hartley, John Hancock, Graham Rees, George Harwood. Front row: Graham Jones, Jack Brennan, Terry Dunn, Les Bettinson, Ken Brunt, Arthur Gregory. This is an interesting line-up for several reasons. Rees, who later moved to Swinton, scored the fastest cup final try at Wembley (35 seconds) for St Helens in 1972. Brennan was in Salford's 1969 Wembley team in his tenth season at the club. Bettinson coached the Red Devils to two championships in the 1970s and later joined the board of directors. Gregory was the father of future Lance Todd Trophy winner and Salford coach Andy Gregory. Hancock was an ex-England Rugby Union international forward.

MANCHESTER XIII	NEW ZEALAND
(White Jerseys)	(Black)
1. K. GOWERS (Swinton)	1. J. E. FAGAN
2. G. JONES (Salford)	4. B. T. REIDY
3. J. CHESHIRE (Salford)	9. R. W. BAILEY
4. P. SMETHURST (Swinton)	7. R. S. COOKE
5. J. STOPFORD (Swinton)	5. A. N. AMER
6. G. PARKINSON (Capt) (Swinton)	10. K. R. McCRACKEN or 13. W. L. SNOWDEN
7. J. BRENNAN (Salford)	14. G. S. FARRAR
8. A. THOMPSON (Swinton)	25. J. R. BUTTERFIELD
9. T. ROBERTS (Swinton)	26. J. G. PATTERSON
10. H. COUNCIL (Salford)	22. H. K. EMERY
11. K. ROBERTS (Swinton)	18. R. D. HAMMOND
12. H. DUFFY (Salford)	24. N. T. TILLER or 15. M. L. COOKE
13. G. REES (Salford)	16. B. E. CASTLE

Referee : Mr. C. F. APPLETON of Warrington.
Touch Judges: Mr. F. Whiteley (Maroon); Mr. W. Fitzhenry (Yellow)

DIRECTORS' REPORT

To the Shareholders of the Salford Football Club Co. (1914) Ltd.

The Directors regret that it is necessary to report the death of Mr. C. M. Webster whose tragic accident was a great shock to everyone and Mr. F. Edwards whose health had been failing for some years. In addition, Mr. W. S. Thomas, our recent ex-chairman, passed away following the completion of more than fifty years of active and loyal service to Salford Football Club.

The Directors submit for your approval the Fiftieth Annual Report and the Accounts and Balance Sheet for the year ended 31st May, 1964, showing a loss of £372 compared with a profit of £1,544 in the previous year.

The 1963-64 Season was most disappointing and the poor performances were sharply reflected in inadequate gate receipts and reduced revenue from the Reconstruction Society.

It would be foolish to anticipate any startling improvement in the immediate future because the present financial situation will only allow meagre expenditure on the signing of new players and therefore only a realistic approach can be the basis for survival.

Upon the resignation of Mr. Jack Lewis it was decided to appoint Mr. Griff Jenkins as Secretary-Coach and it is hoped that his considerable experience in the Coaching field will result in getting better performances from our playing material. In addition, the judicious signing of junior players could provide greater stability at lesser expense than the accepted policy of signing expensive players from other clubs or from Rugby Union sources.

The pursuit of this long term policy cannot be expected to produce immediate results but we are confident that our supporters will always be pleased to acclaim any display of youthful enthusiasm and endeavour.

In an effort to produce more revenue the Directors have been pleased to give their help and assistance to the new and active Supporters Club who are negotiating with Messrs. Groves and Whitnall for the erection of a Social Centre at the Ground. It is hoped that building will be completed before the end of the 1964-65 season and this will provide a new source of revenue with an unlimited potential.

Finally, the Directors have completed arrangements with International Football Pools for the Club to become main agents for this new project which has already received similar support from many of the Rugby League, Association Football and County Cricket Clubs.

We hope that all these progressive plans for 1964-65 will prove successful and help to re-establish the Club on a much stronger basis for the future.

The retiring Directors, Messrs. J. W. Hammond and R. W. Ashworth offer themselves for re-election.

By order of the Board,
G. B. SNAPE, *Chairman.*

In a unique match played at Swinton on 23 August 1961, a combined Salford and Swinton team took on the New Zealand tourists. The result was a 19-7 victory for the 'Manchester' select. The team sheet from the match programme indicates a fair split from the two clubs, although Swinton were a much stronger side at the time. The attendance was 6,926.

The Directors' Report issued with the account statement for the 1963/64 season. Brian Snape had just taken over as chairman in 1963 and was set to make his mark. A few interesting items are included in his report – the pessimistic view that survival was the only realistic approach at this time, the key appointment of Griff Jenkins as the new secretary and coach and the news of a social centre at the ground. Coach Jenkins had his critics, but he made a significant contribution to the club's climb up the table during the late 1960s, culminating in a trip to Wembley in 1969.

Six

The Snape Era
1965-1981

In the mid-1960s Salford quietly, but steadily, climbed the championship table until in 1968/69 they finished sixth. This was the highest position since their fifth placing in 1949/50. It was also the season when Salford returned to Wembley after a thirty-year gap. The reason for the change in fortune could be summed up very quickly – Brian Snape! Here, we see Snape leading out his Salford side at Wembley in 1969, followed by team captain David Watkins, Ken Gwilliam, Bill Burgess, Stuart Whitehead and Chris Hesketh.

Brian Snape was elected to the Salford board of directors in 1960, following in the footsteps of his father Alfred, a board member during the 1930s. He succeeded Jim Hammond as chairman in September 1963. A forward-thinking man, Snape saw his ambition for the club bearing fruit before the decade was over. He recruited stars from both Rugby Union and Rugby League as the team built a reputation for exciting and entertaining rugby. The off-field activities were just as dramatic and in 1966 floodlit rugby arrived, quickly followed by the opening of the Willows Variety Centre. Snape was elected as chairman of the Rugby Football League in 1974 and was to play a major role in several initiatives that took the game forward during the 1970s.

The Willows Variety Centre, pictured before an evening match under the glare of the floodlights. Such was the initial impact, when it first opened under the name of The Salford Football and Social Club on 16 June 1966, that you had to be early to be sure of getting a seat in the club as queues often formed in Willows Road to get in. One of the original compères was Ron Tierney, who did such a wonderful and professional job as the Salford matchday announcer for many years. The floodlights were premiered in a Friday evening fixture with Widnes on 11 March and, for the years that followed, Friday night in Salford was most definitely 'rugby night'.

The signing of David Watkins, the former British Lion and Wales Rugby Union fly-half in October 1967 for a reported £16,000 signing-on fee created sporting headlines and his debut match, at home to Oldham on 20 October, attracted a crowd of 10,117. After several seasons in which he struggled to adapt to the stand-off role, Salford coach Cliff Evans switched him to centre three-quarter. What had seemed an unlikely move paid off handsomely. The extra space out wide meant that his exceptional pace and sidestep were used to a much greater effect. He played 407 times for Salford and claimed several notable individual records. He broke the club goal and point scoring records for a season three times and set a world record of 221 goals in 1972/73. His total of 1,241 goals and 2,907 points are both career records for Salford, overtaking Gus Risman's figures by some distance. He was the captain of Salford at Wembley in 1969 and also when they captured the 1973/74 championship. A tourist in 1974, he was later awarded the MBE.

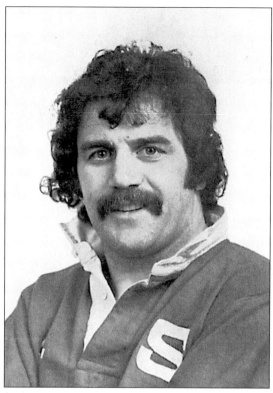

Chris Hesketh arrived at Salford in the summer of 1967 from Wigan, where he had struggled to hold down a first team place, although he was on the substitute bench for them in the 1966 Rugby League Challenge Cup final at Wembley. At Salford, he really blossomed as an exciting centre three-quarter and the fans dubbed him 'Wriggler' because he was so difficult to tackle as he dodged and spun his way through the opposition. Hesketh played 452 times for Salford and his 23 appearances for Great Britain are a record for a Salford player. He toured Australia and New Zealand in 1970 and 1974, being captain on the second occasion. He was also the club captain when Salford secured their second championship of the decade in 1975/76. Like Watkins, he was later honoured with the MBE.

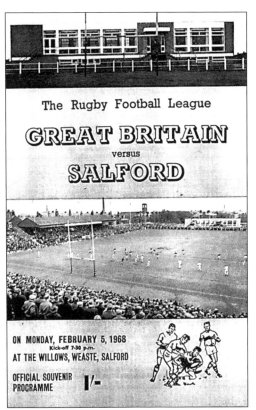

The Willows was the place to be in the late 1960s and the Red Devils even took on the Great Britain team on 5 February 1968. The match was organised to allow the national side to play together in preparation for the upcoming World Cup tournament in Australia; 4,500 hardy souls turned out in a snowstorm for a match that was finally abandoned after 35 minutes with Great Britain 12-0 in front. The match was restaged at Salford on 5 April 1968, when Great Britain won 20-5.

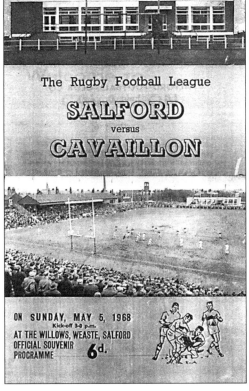

The first Sunday match played at The Willows was against the touring French club side, Cavaillon, on 5 May 1968. Salford won with ease by 43-10 against a very lightweight French pack. Salford's average attendance for the 1967/68 season was 7,332. This was well up on the 4,441 for the previous campaign and more than double the average of 3,382 from two seasons earlier.

The powerful second row forward Mike Coulman in action for Great Britain against France at St Helens on 17 March 1971. Coulman, an England Rugby Union international, signed for Salford from Moseley Rugby Union Club in October 1968 for a fee of £8,500. He went on to play 463 matches for Salford and his 135 tries is a record for a Salford forward. Extremely fast for his size, it was very difficult for opponents to bring him down once he was into his stride. He later became the coach at Salford for a short period during the 1983/84 season.

Salford sign Burgess and go for Dixon

DOUBLE DEAL WILL BE £20,000 RECORD

SALFORD today signed Barrow's Test winger Bill Burgess in the first leg of what will be the biggest double signing deal in Rugby League history.

After securing Burgess's signature, chairman Brian Snape was dashing to Halifax in a bid to sign Test second-rower Colin Dixon. The two signings could cost Salford close on £20,000.

Burgess makes his debut in tmorrow night's home match against Wakefield Trinity and Salford were hoping Dixon would also be in the team.

It is believed that Burgess cost Salford about £6,000 while Dixon was expected to mean a payout of over £10,000 plus winger Mike Kelly.

Kelly, valued by Salford at £3,500, is being interviewed tonight by Halifax. The clubs have already agreed terms.

A fortnight ago 29-year-old Burgess said he was retiring, after scoring three dazzling tries for Great Britain against France. He later had second thoughts.

ACCOMPLISHED

Burgess is still one of the code's most accomplished wings and has played 13 times for Britain as well as touring Australia and New Zealand in 1966.

Dixon, aged 25, is a former Cardiff junior RU player. He joined Halifax as a centre in 1961.

● BILL BURGESS

£50,000 SPREE

HERE is a list of Salford's spending spree over the past three seasons. Before today's deals they had paid out about £50,000 in transfer and signing fees.

David Watkins	£13,000
Arthur Hughes	£5,000
Mike Coulman	£5,000
Peter Smethurst	£3,000
Malcolm Price	£2,000
Jim Mills	£3,000
Mike Kelly	£3,000
Ken Halliwell	£3,000
Alan McInnes	£4,000
Chris Hesketh	£4,000
Charlie Bott	£3,000
David Evans	£2,000

Salford had already made the headlines by signing international Rugby Union stars David Watkins and Mike Coulman but, on Thursday 19 December 1968, it became clear that chairman Brian Snape really meant business. This exciting splash in the *Manchester Evening News* announced the capture of two current Great Britain Rugby League internationals – wing three-quarter Bill Burgess from Barrow for a £6,000 transfer fee, and the imminent arrival of Halifax's Colin Dixon. Burgess was one of the most graceful wingers ever to wear the red jersey of Salford but, unfortunately, a persistent shoulder injury forced his retirement in 1970 after just 44 matches for the club.

Colin Dixon was the second part of Salford's great double signing. The Welshman, who started his rugby career as a three-quarter, had already appeared in two championship finals with Halifax and was now making his name as a back row forward. It had taken a Rugby League record transfer fee of £11,500 to persuade Halifax to part with him. He was a strong running, ball-playing forward and, like Burgess, was a member of the 1969 Wembley line-up. He went on to play 418 times for Salford.

THE RUGBY LEAGUE CHALLENGE CUP COMPETITION
FINAL
SATURDAY MAY 17th, 1969 Kick-off 3p.m.

CASTLEFORD V SALFORD

Official Programme Two Shillings

EMPIRE WEMBLEY STADIUM

The Rugby League Challenge Cup final against Castleford on 17 May 1969 drew the second highest crowd ever seen at Wembley for a Rugby League match (97,939). Although Salford lost to their bogey side of the period, most supporters were just happy to see the club back in the final after thirty years absence, anticipating a speedy and more successful return. Few would have thought that it would be Salford's last Wembley visit of the twentieth century.

Salford's 1969 Wembley squad. From left to right, back row: Alan McInnes (in club blazer), Bill Burgess, Colin Dixon, Stuart Whitehead, Terry Ogden, Mike Coulman, Ron Hill, Charlie Bott, Griff Jenkins (secretary/coach). Middle row: Martin Dickens, Paul Jackson, Jack Brennan, Brian Snape (chairman), David Watkins (captain), Chris Hesketh, Ken Gwilliam. Front row (kneeling): Peter Smethurst, Trevor Rabbitt. On the day of the big match, Salford's Welsh scrum-half Bob Prosser was preferred on the substitute bench ahead of a disappointed Rabbitt.

Classy winger Bill Burgess makes a break down the right flank for Salford at Wembley. It was to be a disappointing game for the great player, being injured in almost the first move of the match and experiencing Wembley defeat for the second time, having lost with Barrow two years earlier.

Chris Hesketh splits the Castleford defence during the cup final in a move that led to him touching down just before half-time. As Salford led 4-3 at that time, it would have been a crucial score but, unfortunately, the referee disallowed the 'try' for a 'double movement' by Hesketh. It was to be the closest that Salford came to crossing the opposition line all afternoon.

Left winger Maurice Richards was another major capture from Welsh Rugby Union circles in October 1969, when he was signed for a reported £7,000 fee from Cardiff. The former British Lion had gained instant fame when he scored a record-breaking four tries for Wales against England the previous April. Richards was a great favourite at Salford where his strong running and deceptive side step allowed him to escape the clutches of opponents even when he had very little space to operate in. He is the holder of two major individual club records at Salford: the most games ever played (498) and the most tries scored (297). He was a Great Britain tourist in 1974.

The signing of Paul Charlton created a new Rugby League transfer record when he arrived from Workington Town for £12,500 in October 1969. Rated by many as the finest full-back in the game at the time, he was virtually overlooked for international selection until he came into the limelight with Salford. Whilst at Salford, he played 18 times for Great Britain to add to his solitary 1965 appearance and he was also a tourist in 1974. He was not in the traditional mould of kicking full-backs but, nonetheless, he was one of the most reliable and effective tacklers ever seen in the game. His trademark of linking up with the three-quarter line turned him into a potent attacking force and produced a Rugby League record of 33 tries by a full-back in 1972/73. He made 234 appearances for Salford before returning to Workington as their coach in 1975.

The arrival of Cliff Evans as club coach in May 1970 was a turning point for the team. He had already achieved success with Swinton and St Helens and, at Salford, he took over a side that was already blessed with great individual skill and welded it into a cohesive unit. In February 1971, his promotion of the youthful half-back pairing of Ken Gill and Peter Banner into the first team and the relocation of David Watkins to the three-quarter line was an inspired move. Ill health forced Evans to retire midway through the 1973/74 championship season, but much of the credit for that success rests on his shoulders.

Ken Gill in typical action as he looks to offload the ball. Gill was a creative ball-playing stand-off, who carved openings for colleagues out of seemingly nothing, rarely running through gaps himself. His kicks into the corner for flying wingman Keith Fielding to chase, and usually recover, was a particularly lethal weapon in the team's armoury. Gill was a Great Britain tourist in 1974 and his 12 appearances for England is second only to George Curran amongst Salford players. Interestingly, this picture features two future Salford coaches: Widnes's Mal Aspey (in white jersey, next to referee Fred Lindop) and Salford's Kevin Ashcroft (on the ground). This scene is from the John Player Trophy semi-final against Widnes at Warrington on 3 November 1979, which Salford lost 19-3.

Salford broke the Rugby League transfer record once again when Eric Prescott arrived from St Helens for £13,500 in September 1972. A loose forward noted for his tough and uncompromising tackling, his signing considerably strengthened the Red Devils' defensive line. He made 273 appearances for Salford before he transferred to Widnes in September 1980. It was a move that paid off personally and he was to experience two Wembley cup finals with Widnes before returning to Salford in 1984, when he played in a further 18 matches.

The former England Rugby Union winger Keith Fielding was probably the fastest player ever on Salford's books. He was extremely quick off the mark and once in space no one could catch him. Signed from Moseley Rugby Union Club for £8,500 in May 1973, he broke the club's forty-year-old try scoring record with 46 touchdowns in his debut season. He also played in his first international match that season for Great Britain, where a spectacular hat-trick of tries against France in Grenoble earned him the title of 'Le Rapide'. He played 319 times for Salford and registered 253 tries. Towards the end of his rugby playing days he achieved national fame through his success in BBC television's *Superstars* series.

Great Britain international scrum-half Steve Nash was signed from Featherstone Rovers in August 1975. For the fourth consecutive time, Salford set a new Rugby League transfer record, handing over a £15,000 fee. Nash had been to Wembley twice with the Rovers and was voted Lance Todd Trophy winner in 1973 as the man of the match. Sadly, he was unable to make a return visit to the famous stadium in Salford colours. A powerful scrum-half, he was always in the thick of the action and just as happy to mix it with the opposing forwards as he was with the backs. He played 275 times for Salford. In this picture, he attempts to tackle his opposite number, Reg Bowden of Widnes, whilst colleagues Chris McGreal (left) and Colin Dixon look on.

John Butler, a Great Britain tourist in 1974, was signed from Rochdale Hornets in March 1975 for £7,000. He shared in Salford's championship success of 1975/76, playing in the Premiership final against St Helens during the same season. An elusive player, who appeared to glide past defenders, he played 135 times for the Red Devils.

One of the most dramatic post-war changes to the ground was the erection of the imposing North Stand at the cricket ground end. Here, we see the early stages of construction taking place. Unfortunately, the development meant that the row of trees, which had long provided a picturesque backdrop between the rugby and cricket grounds over the years, was no longer visible.

An artist's impression of the North Stand, which seats 1,650 spectators, before it was completed in the summer of 1971. It was intended to add further seating to the area in front of the stand, but this never happened. This is the reason why the terrace steps are so steep at that part of the ground.

An opportunity for further development arose after the centre section of the Main Stand caught fire on 26 November 1972. The blaze was first noticed a few hours after Salford had entertained Workington Town, suggesting that a discarded cigarette could have been the cause. It was decided to reconstruct the centre section with the addition of a High Level Stand. This picture captures the first phase of the construction work.

The High Level Stand, which was finished in time for the 1973/74 season, is now predominantly used by directors, officials and sponsors of the club. This picture, taken in 1980, clearly illustrates the panoramic view it affords.

The Lancashire Challenge Cup final victory in 1972 was Salford's first trophy success since 1939. The Red Devils defeated Swinton 25-11 at Warrington. The disappointing attendance of 6,865 was blamed on the live television coverage of the match by BBC's *Grandstand* programme.

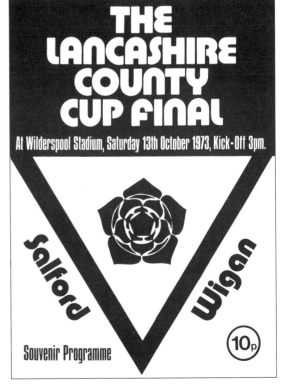

Salford returned to defend the Lancashire Cup in the 1973 final, also played at Warrington, but unexpectedly lost to Wigan 19-9.

A third consecutive Lancashire Cup final appearance, in 1974, was played at Wigan's Central Park ground. Widnes, just embarking on what would prove to be a successful era for the club, won narrowly by 6-2. Salford were badly handicapped by the late withdrawals, through injury, of international backs Chris Hesketh and Ken Gill. One consolation was the outstanding display by second row forward Mike Coulman who took the *Rugby Leaguer* man of the match award.

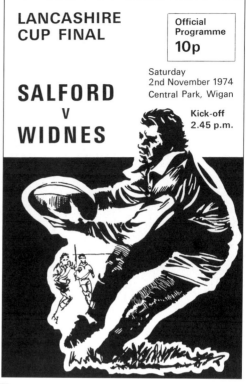

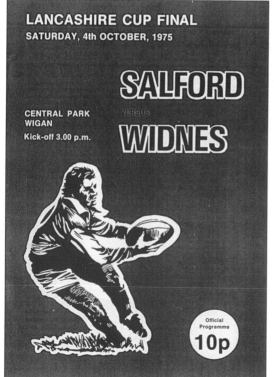

In 1975, Salford made a club-record fourth successive Lancashire Cup final appearance, surpassing the three in a row they made during 1934, 1935 and 1936. Unfortunately, they lost for the third year running and, once again, Widnes were the victors with a scoreline of 16-7. The final, staged at Wigan, was played throughout in a torrential downpour, which made for heavy conditions.

THE TEAMS

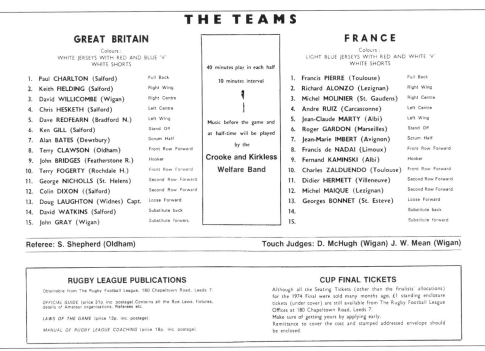

GREAT BRITAIN				FRANCE	
Colours: WHITE JERSEYS WITH RED AND BLUE 'V' WHITE SHORTS				Colours: LIGHT BLUE JERSEYS WITH RED AND WHITE 'V' WHITE SHORTS	

Centre panel:
40 minutes play in each half

10 minutes interval

Music before the game and at half-time will be played by the

Crooke and Kirkless Welfare Band

GREAT BRITAIN			FRANCE	
1.	Paul CHARLTON (Salford)	Full Back	1.	Francis PIERRE (Toulouse)	Full Back
2.	Keith FIELDING (Salford)	Right Wing	2.	Richard ALONZO (Lezignan)	Right Wing
3.	David WILLICOMBE (Wigan)	Right Centre	3.	Michel MOLINIER (St. Gaudens)	Right Centre
4.	Chris HESKETH (Salford)	Left Centre	4.	Andre RUIZ (Carcassonne)	Left Centre
5.	Dave REDFEARN (Bradford N.)	Left Wing	5.	Jean-Claude MARTY (Albi)	Left Wing
6.	Ken GILL (Salford)	Stand Off	6.	Roger GARDON (Marseilles)	Stand Off
7.	Alan BATES (Dewsbury)	Scrum Half	7.	Jean-Marie IMBERT (Avignon)	Scrum Half
8.	Terry CLAWSON (Oldham)	Front Row Forward	8.	Francis de NADAI (Limoux)	Front Row Forward
9.	John BRIDGES (Featherstone R.)	Hooker	9.	Fernand KAMINSKI (Albi)	Hooker
10.	Terry FOGERTY (Rochdale H.)	Front Row Forward	10.	Charles ZALDUENDO (Toulouse)	Front Row Forward
11.	George NICHOLLS (St. Helens)	Second Row Forward	11.	Didier HERMETT (Villeneuve)	Second Row Forward
12.	Colin DIXON ((Salford)	Second Row Forward	12.	Michel MAIQUE (Lezignan)	Second Row Forward
13.	Doug LAUGHTON (Widnes) Capt.	Loose Forward	13.	Georges BONNET (St. Esteve)	Loose Forward
14.	David WATKINS (Salford)	Substitute back	14.		Substitute back
15.	John GRAY (Wigan)	Substitute forward	15.		Substitute forward

Referee: S. Shepherd (Oldham) Touch Judges: D. McHugh (Wigan) J. W. Mean (Wigan)

RUGBY LEAGUE PUBLICATIONS

Obtainable from The Rugby Football League, 180 Chapeltown Road, Leeds 7.

OFFICIAL GUIDE (price 31p. inc. postage).Contains all the Bye Laws, fixtures, details of Amateur organisations, Referees etc.

LAWS OF THE GAME (price 13p. inc. postage).

MANUAL OF RUGBY LEAGUE COACHING (price 18p. inc. postage).

CUP FINAL TICKETS

Although all the Seating Tickets (other than the finalists' allocations) for the 1974 Final were sold many months ago, £1 standing enclosure tickets (under cover) are still available from The Rugby Football League Offices at 180 Chapeltown Road, Leeds 7. Make sure of getting yours by applying early. Remittance to cover the cost and stamped addressed envelope should be enclosed.

Salford's strength can be gauged from this Great Britain line-up to face France at Wigan on 12 February 1974, when they won 29-0. The selection of six Salford players equalled the club record established the previous month when France were defeated 24-5 at Grenoble. The same six took part in both matches. The previous best for Salford had been five during the 1930s.

The Salford Championship winning team of 1973/74. From left to right, back row: Coulman, Prescott, Grice, MacKay, Bettinson (coach), Dixon, Knighton, Davies, Fielding, Richards, Evans (former coach). Front row: Walker, Gill, Charlton, Hesketh, Snape (chairman), Watkins (captain), Hammond (president), Banner, Taylor. The season saw a return to two divisions with no end-of-season play-off. Salford clinched the title by topping the table after a nail-biting finale over Easter. The Red Devils dramatically won at Wigan 21-12 on Easter Monday afternoon in their final game to leapfrog St Helens, who then lost at Widnes in the evening. This picture was taken on 21 April 1974, prior to the short-lived Club Championship end-of-season play-off with Bradford at The Willows. A crowd of 10,236 saw the club presented with their first championship trophy in thirty-five years.

Salford's six 1974 tourists pictured at the Sydney Cricket Ground, the venue for so many famous Rugby League Test matches over the years. From left to right, back row: Paul Charlton, Chris Hesketh, Colin Dixon, Maurice Richards. Front row: Ken Gill, David Watkins. It was a record representation from the club for a tour, beating the previous high of five picked for the 1936 party. Hesketh's selection as tour captain was the third time that a Salford player had been honoured in this way, following in the footsteps of Jimmy Lomas (1910) and Gus Risman (1946). All six players played in Test matches and in one of them, the Third Test against Australia at Sydney on 20 July, five appeared together – Charlton, Dixon, Gill, Hesketh and Richards. Australia won that match 22-18 to clinch the series 2-1. This was after Britain had tied the rubber with a 16-11 win at the same ground in the Second Test when tour captain Hesketh had been carried triumphantly from the field. Despite this setback, the tourists lifted themselves for the New Zealand leg, winning 20-0 in the deciding Auckland Test after Hesketh had pushed his team for one final effort at the end of a tough three-month schedule.

In December 1974, Salford made it through to the final of the BBC2 Floodlit Trophy final for the only time. Matches in this competition, which ran from 1965 until 1979, were played, one per week, live on the BBC2 television channel. Salford's opposition was Warrington, themselves making their only final appearance in the competition. The Red Devils failed to cash in on the luck of having a home tie and were held to a scoreless draw at The Willows.

For the only time in the competition's history, the BBC2 Floodlit Trophy final went to a replay. This was staged at Warrington on a wet and muddy evening on 28 January 1975. David Watkins and Keith Fielding combined to score a remarkable try in only the sixth minute that set Salford on course for victory. Catching a missed penalty kick near the posts, Watkins sprinted the length of the field down the right flank before sending Fielding in from the halfway line. A foul by a Warrington defender on Fielding, as he touched down, meant the Reds were also awarded a penalty kick after the try had been converted, for a 7-0 lead.

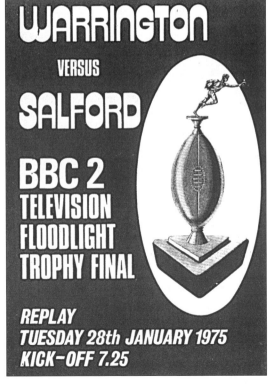

Jubilant Salford captain, Chris Hesketh, is chaired from the field by his team after the BBC2 Floodlit Trophy victory over Warrington. The final score was 10-5.

Dressing room celebrations for captain Chris Hesketh (centre) and his muddied but happy Floodlit Trophy heroes.

Salford players picked for the England and Wales squads during a photocall at The Willows before setting off for Australia and New Zealand for the 1975 World Cup series. From left to right, back row: Coulman (England), Dixon (Wales). Front row: Watkins (Wales), Gill (England), Banner (Wales), Fielding (England). Banner, from Rochdale in Lancashire, qualified for Wales through his parentage. The Welsh manager Les Pearce can be seen in the background (centre, arms folded).

The 1975/76 Salford Championship winning side. From left to right, back row: Coulman, Corcoran, Sheffield, Dixon, Turnbull, Prescott, Grice, Knighton, Stead, Frodsham, Richards. Front row: Watkins, Butler, Nash, Hesketh (captain), Snape (chairman), Bettinson (coach), Graham, Fielding, Raistrick. This picture was taken at The Willows on 30 April 1976 when Salford were presented with the championship trophy before the first round Premiership Trophy play-off against Hull KR.

THE TEAMS

ST. HELENS 3-3-15

Colours:
White Jerseys with Red "V", White Shorts

Coach: ERIC ASHTON M.B.E.

1.	GEOFF PIMBLETT (3 goals)	Full Back
2.	LES JONES	Right Wing
3.	~~EDDIE CUNNINGHAM~~ PETER GLYNN (Try)	Right Centre
4.	DEREK NOONAN	Left Centre
5.	ROY MATHIAS	Left Wing
6.	BILLY BENYON	Stand Off
7.	JEFF HEATON	Scrum Half
8.	JOHN MANTLE	Front Row Forward
9.	TONY KARALIUS (Try)	Hooker
10.	~~KEL COSLETT (Captain)~~ MEL JAMES	Front Row Forward
11.	GEORGE NICHOLLS	Second Row Forward
12.	ERIC CHISNALL (Try)	Second Row Forward
13.	~~DAVID HULL~~ KEL COSLETT	Loose Forward
14.	~~PETER GLYNN~~ KEN GWILLIAM (for Heaton 50 mn)	Substitute Back
15.	~~MEL JAMES~~ HARRY PINNER	Substitute Forward

H - T . 0 - 1

SALFORD 2-0-2

Colours:
Red Jerseys, White Shorts

Coach: LES BETTINSON

1.	DAVID WATKINS (2 drop goals)	Full Back
2.	KEITH FIELDING	Right Wing
3.	CHRIS HESKETH	Right Centre
4.	MAURICE RICHARDS	Left Centre
5.	GORDON GRAHAM	Left Wing
6.	JOHN BUTLER	Stand Off
7.	STEVE NASH	Scrum Half
8.	MIKE COULMAN	Front Row Forward
9.	DEAN RAISTRICK	Hooker
10.	BILL SHEFFIELD	Front Row Forward
11.	JOHN KNIGHTON	Second Row Forward
12.	COLIN DIXON	Second Row Forward
13.	ERIC PRESCOTT	Loose Forward
14.	~~JOHN RAWLINSON~~ SAM TURNBULL (for Knighton 70 mn)	Substitute Back
15.	ALAN GRICE	Substitute Forward

ATT: 18,008

RL

Today's Chief Guest, the Rt. Hon. The Earl of Derby, M.C., President of the Rugby Football League, will present the Premiership Trophy. The teams will be presented to Lord Derby and Mr. Harry Womersley, Vice-Chairman of the Rugby Football League, before the kick off.

The replay, if necessary, will be staged on Wednesday, May 26, 1976, at Station Road, Swinton, kick off 7.30 p.m.

Quiz Answers: 1. Hull K.R. and Wigan; 2. W. H. Thompson (Leeds); 3. Mel Mason (Huddersfield); 4. Granada Television.

Referee: M. J. NAUGHTON (Widnes)   Touch Judges: W. FIDDES (Rodley) F. J. TOMLINSON (Widnes)

The 1976 Premiership Trophy final, played at Swinton, saw Salford, the newly crowned Rugby League champions, pitted against St Helens, the Challenge Cup winners. Both paraded their trophies before the match in front of a (then) record Premiership Trophy final crowd of 18,000.

A key moment in the 1976 Premiership Trophy final as St Helens centre Peter Glynn dives between Salford skipper Chris Hesketh (4) and Colin Dixon to score. The scoreboard at the back shows 2-2 but the Saints, inspired by Glynn's sixty-eighth-minute try, finished strongly to win 15-2.

105

The Salford team who played in the 1979 centenary match against Widnes on 14 October. From left to right, back row: Mike Coulman, Sam Turnbull, Stewart Williams, Colin Dixon, Chris McGreal, Eric Prescott, David Stephenson, Frank Wilson, Maurice Richards. Front row: David Harris, Ken Gill, Keith Fielding, Paul O'Neill, Colin Whitfield, Steve Rule. The players wore red, amber and black hoops, the original colours of the club until 1883, when the famous red shirt appeared.

Salford captain Keith Fielding, accompanied by the club mascot, leads out his team for the centenary match in front of a club-record Division One crowd of 11,982. Brian Snape proudly follows his brother Keith (out of shot) who had taken over as chairman of the club the previous year. Widnes had been the opposition for Salford's first home match on 11 October 1879. Fielding was to grab the Red Devils' opening try whilst David Stephenson, just behind him, scored a second-half drop goal which had given Salford what looked like a winning 14-8 lead before Widnes rallied.

Salford second row forward Stewart Williams (right) assists an unidentifiable colleague to halt the progress of Widnes' Welsh prop Glyn Shaw during the centenary match.

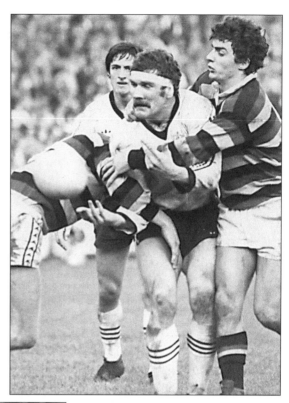

Steve Rule about to kick one of his four place goals (he also added a drop goal). His late penalty goal left the centenary match all square at 16-16. Rule's 13 goals in a match against Doncaster in 1981 equalled the club record, which he still shares with Gus Risman (1933 and 1940) and David Watkins (1972).

In the late 1970s, several of Salford's greatest players of the previous decade received testimonials in recognition of their services to the club. The first was a joint effort for Chris Hesketh (left) and David Watkins (second from right) in 1978. The two players are seen here with the famous local artist Harold Riley (a keen follower of Rugby League) and Tom Bergin (right). Bergin was a renowned journalist who covered Salford Rugby League affairs in the *Salford City Reporter* for over fifty years. He was, for many years, the chairman of the Rugby League Writers Association and, in 1987, was honoured with the inauguration of The Tom Bergin Trophy, presented to the man of the match in the Second Division Premiership Trophy final.

Forwards Mike Coulman (left) and Colin Dixon (right) were the next pair to share a testimonial, in 1979. As it concluded, they were able to point to Maurice Richards (centre) as the next recipient in 1980. Whilst it was fitting that these great players were being rewarded for their wonderful service to the club, it also signalled the end of an era as their glittering playing careers were coming to a finish. It was a warning of declining fortunes to come.

Keith Snape took over as chairman, from his brother Brian, in 1978. This picture, at a snow-covered Willows ground, was taken in January 1979 when most of the Rugby League fixtures were wiped out for a month. The chairman appears to be asking: 'What can I do about the weather?' The North Stand dominates the cricket ground end in the background.

A break in play as Salford front row forwards Harold Henney, Paul O'Neill and Tony Gourley wait to pack down at a scrum. In the background, from the left, are Colin Dixon, Steve Rule, Colin Whitfield and Sam Turnbull. This picture was taken during the 1979/80 season.

Salford at home to Leigh in the first match of the season on 17 August 1980. Stand-off half Frank Wilson prepares to offload to the supporting Colin Whitfield as full-back Frank Stead watches in the background. The occasion was a first round Lancashire Cup-tie, which the Red Devils won 23-12.

Salford visited Oldham for the second round of the 1980 Lancashire Cup on 24 August. Prop forward Harold Henney, who normally played in the second row, appears to be taking on the whole of the Oldham team. Unfortunately, it was to no avail, as Salford narrowly lost 13-15. Henney, a powerful running Cumbrian forward had been signed from Workington Town for £4,000 in January 1978.

Seven

The Wilkinson Years
1982-2000

On 3 January 1982, before the home match with Oldham, it was announced that John Wilkinson was the new chairman of Salford Rugby League Football Club. The previous decade had been one of the most exciting in the history of the club but, with mounting debts and poor on-field performances leading to relegation into the Second Division, the new chairman knew he had a challenge on his hands. Whilst the glory days were not instantly recaptured, progress was steady under the new chairman and, by the start of the new millennium, the renamed Salford City Reds had firmly established themselves in the elite new world of Super League. This picture captures the after-match jubilation as Salford players (left to right) Paul Forber, Andy Burgess (holding up the trophy) and Nathan McAvoy celebrate winning the Divisional Premiership final in 1996. It was the second time during the decade that Salford had captured the trophy.

John Wilkinson was, at the beginning of year 2000, the longest serving club chairman in British Rugby League, with eighteen years at the helm of Salford Rugby League Club. Initially a supporter of rivals Swinton, his interest and enthusiasm for Salford had developed during 1968 with the arrival of David Watkins and the era of Friday night rugby at The Willows. A successful businessman, he sponsored the club on numerous occasions before making the bold decision to take a controlling interest in 1982. During the period of his chairmanship he has had to endure some very testing times. The compliance to the Safety of Sports Grounds Act was a major, although necessary, drain on the club as were repairs to damage that affected, in particular, both the North and Main stands. Progress on the playing front was slow as Wilkinson strove to put the club into the black. After a 'yo-yo' period that saw the team relegated four times between 1981 and 1995, stability was achieved in 1996 when promotion to the Super League was secured. A further positive step was the recent reacquisition of the Willows Variety Centre, which had previously been sold to Greenall Whitley in 1980 to reduce overheads. An amiable but shrewd chairman, Wilkinson has always adopted a hands-on approach, involving himself in most aspects of the club's affairs.

Salford second row forward Ronnie Smith touches down for a try in the Second Division clash against Fulham at The Willows on 26 September 1982. Although the London side eventually won 26-13, Salford still achieved promotion in John Wilkinson's first full season as chairman. The other Salford players are, from left to right: Keith Fielding (at the back), Sam Turnbull and Trevor Stockley.

Harold Henney makes a powerful break for Salford as he exploits a gap in the Keighley defence. Racing up in support is stand-off half Ged Byrne. Salford won this match, played at The Willows on 20 February 1983, by 20-11.

XIII CATALAN

GAZETTE SAISON 1983-84

Match International de jeu à XIII

DIMANCHE 1er AVRIL 1984   **SALFORD**

STADE GILBERT-BRUTUS   contre

PERPIGNAN — 15 h 30   **XIII CATALAN**

13 HEURES MATCH D'OUVERTURE

Fifty years after the historic pioneering tour of France in 1934, Salford was invited back to commemorate half a century of Rugby League in that country with a match against XIII Catalan of Perpignan. Two of the original Red Devils, Gus Risman and Emlyn Jenkins, joined the official Salford party for an emotional reunion with former adversaries.

CINQUANTENAIRE

du

XIII CATALAN

———

Chapelle Saint-Dominique

Rue Rabelais, Perpignan

Soirée
de
Gala

Samedi 31 mars 1984

On the eve of the match against XIII Catalan, the Salford players and officials were honoured with a 'Soirée de Gala' on 31 March 1984. Illustrated here is the cover from a special dinner menu produced to mark the occasion.

Salford's match with XIII Catalan took place on 1 April 1984, almost exactly fifty years after the two clubs had first met. Here, second row forward Stewart Williams prepares to pass to the supporting Peter Glynn (4). The French side eventually won 8-7.

Unfortunately, poor conditions for the match against XIII Catalan saw the pitch deteriorate into a mud bath. Here, scrum-half Darren Bloor, who contributed a drop goal, tries to break away from a mêlée of players that appear to be 'squaring up' to one another in the background. The player on the left is Peter Glynn, who had been such a thorn in Salford's side in the 1976 Premiership Trophy final; he changed his allegiance to the Red Devils in the summer of 1983.

A high profile meeting was organised at the Willows Variety Centre on 3 October 1984, with an open invitation to anyone who cared about the future of the club. Wilkinson is seen here making a heartfelt speech as he outlines the financial plight of the club. During the evening the club launched the 'Lifeline' scheme that was a vital source of income in the years that followed. Listening intently on the front row are the Salford coaching staff of Tom Grainey (left), Kevin Ashcroft and Bob Welding.

Scrum-half Neil Ritter was one of several Australian players signed by Salford for the 1984/85 season. It was the club's first significant foray into that market, a trend that has continued for both Salford and the English game in general over the years since. Ritter is in action against Bridgend at The Willows on 30 September. Salford won convincingly by 64-18. Bridgend were the new incarnation of the Cardiff City team, but lasted only one season before folding. Having been relegated at the end of the previous season, Salford finished second to regain their place in the top division. The other Salford players in the background are John Taylor and New Zealander Roby Muller (with headband).

Salford appeared in their first major final for twelve years when the Lancashire Challenge Cup final was reached in 1988. Under coach Kevin Ashcroft, the team were enjoying their fourth successive season in the First Division, but were up against strong opposition with the holders Wigan. Although beaten 22-17, the Red Devils put up a tough fight and their Australian stand-off, Paul Shaw, won the man of the match award. Played at St Helens, the final attracted a crowd of 19,154.

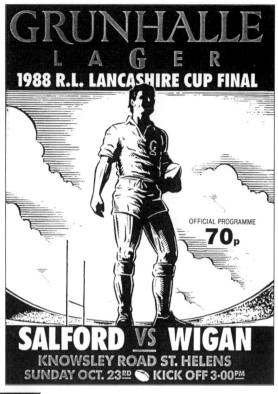

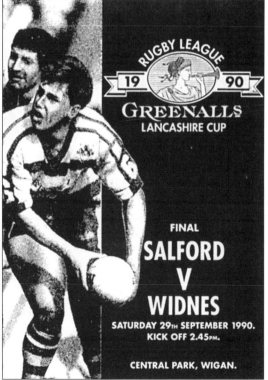

Another Lancashire Cup final appearance came in 1990, this time against Widnes at Central Park, Wigan. Now coached by New Zealander Kevin Tamati, Salford gave a warning of what they were capable of by disposing of three First Division sides on their way to the final. Widnes, destined to be First Division runners-up, were clear favourites but, once more, Salford put on a brave show. They finally lost in the latter stages of the match by 24-18 and again, in defeat, had the man of the match recipient in stand-off half David Fell. Having been relegated once more at the end of the previous season, it was the start of the club's most promising campaign in over a decade.

Salford captain Ian Blease proudly holds up the Second Division Championship Bowl after topping the table for 1990/91. It was the club's first silverware since 1976 and the first success for Salford chairman John Wilkinson. The trophy was presented at The Willows immediately after the Second Division match with Keighley on 14 April 1991. Of the 28 league games played, Salford had lost only once.

Action from the Salford versus Halifax 1991 Second Division Premiership final played at Old Trafford on 12 May. The two clubs had not met during the season, as there were too many teams (21) in the division for a full fixture list. Halifax, as runners-up, naturally saw the final as a chance to prove themselves against the team that had finished above them. Steve Kerry, the Salford scrum-half seen here trying to set up another attack, had an outstanding match and contributed two tries and five goals towards Salford's 27-20 triumph. His performance earned him the Tom Bergin Trophy.

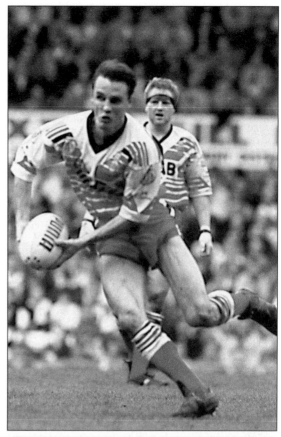

The victorious Salford team, immediately after receiving the 1991 Second Division Premiership Trophy at Old Trafford. From left to right, back row (standing): Terry Cassidy (coaching staff), Mick Worrall, Arthur Bradshaw, Mick Dean, Andy Burgess, Mark Lee, Shane Hansen, Adrian Hadley. Front row (kneeling): Ian Sherratt, John Gilfillan, Ian Blease, Steve Gibson, Tex Evans, Steve Kerry, Martin Birkett, Frank Cassidy.

Salford versus Wigan in a First Division match, played at a packed Willows ground during the 1994/95 season. Salford's Jason Critchley makes the tackle and Welsh wingman Phil Ford (5) prepares to give his support. Salford lost heavily (42-8) in this encounter, which was played on 19 March 1995.

Two ex-Wigan stars, Andy Gregory (left, making the tackle) and Sam Panapa, take on their former colleagues in the Salford versus Wigan clash on 19 March 1995. For Gregory, it was a disappointing second match as the new club coach – having taken over just a few weeks earlier from the ex-Australian international full-back, Garry Jack. At the end of the 1994/95 season, Salford were relegated from the top division, even though they finished twelfth of the sixteen teams, due to a realignment of the divisions to accommodate the creation of the new Super League competition.

WIGAN TOPPLED FROM THEIR PEDESTAL

Super Salford into history

SALFORD'S magnificent, rip-roaring Reds proudly take their place in history after ripping out Wigan's world-record page.

After eight years and 43 Cup tie triumphs, Wigan, winners of the Silk Cut Challenge Cup for the past eight years, were toppled from their pedestal at the joy-filled Willows.

And this was no fluke, no bizarre result when the champions were caught on an off-day. Wigan's star-studded line-up played and fought like the champions they undoubtedly are.

Salford played football of the most supreme quality to outplay, out-tough and outlast their distinguished and, previously, invincible opponents.

It was a triumph of tactics and preparation for coach Andy Gregory and his assistants John Foran and Steve O'Neill, all three of them former Wigan players.

It was a triumph for the 14 Salford heroes who took the pitch. They were men oozing a confidence that had been with them for the past two weeks since they heard the draw for this fifth round tie.

The scenes at the end were amazing. Reds' fans, many with tears in their eyes, hugged each other, others roared their heads off, chanting "We're on our way to Wembley", or that stirring refrain from The Vikings film score, which has become their battle hymn.

Chairman John Wilkinson, the longest-serving in the game, received handshakes and back-slaps, his eyes glazed in pure delight.

And, in one of the most moving and gratifying sights seen on any sports ground, thousands of Wigan fans, packed into the North Stand, rose to give their victors a standing ovation.

But it was a game worthy of such scenes, a pulsating, nerve-tingling epic that rocketed through the 80 minutes like a Startrek trip on the Enterprise.

Stand-off Steve Blakeley, at his breathtaking best, took the Press award as man-of-the match.

By George Dowson

Victory meant something extra-special for Blakeley, a youngster of enormous potential at Wigan who left Central Park because his route to the first team was blocked by the talents of Andy Gregory, Shaun Edwards and Frano Botica.

But there were heroes and candidates for that award all the way through this superb Salford side.

Skipper David Young surely had his best game ever, giving a stirring lead.

His front row partners, Cliff Eccles and Peter Edwards, backed him magnificently.

Salford 26 Wigan 16

Second rower Paul Forber was a giant, a colossus smashing his way through on numerous occasions.

Scrum half Mark Lee tormented Wigan to death with his outstanding tactical kicking and chipped through, in only the fourth minute, to pave the way for Young to dive through for the first try.

In the second half he bamboozled Wigan with an audacious dummy and storming run to send in the excellent Scott Martin for another try.

Alongside Martin, in the centre, Scott Naylor, another ex-Wiganer, crowned his glorious season with two magnificent tries. For Naylor, too, this day was something extra special. He joined Salford from Wigan after battling his way back from a career-threatening injury.

And, at the back, was the rock, Steve Hampson, fearless and steadfast under the high ball, deadly in the tackle and always threatening when he linked in attack.

As another former Central Park hero, who played in five Cup Finals for Wigan, he wanted this victory to exorcise the grudge he had held for two years that chairman Jack Robinson was wrong in letting him go.

STAR MEN: Hampson, McAvoy, Naylor, Martin, Rogers, Blakeley, Lee, Young, Edwards, Eccles, Forber, Savelio, Panapa, Burgess.

■ CRUNCH . . . Tuigamala takes the full force of a Salford attack

■ NO WAY! Salford's Scott Martin tries to burst through

■ MAKE WAY . . . David Young makes the breakthrough

Lindsay leads the praise

TRIBUTES came pouring in to salute Salford's Cup triumph, led by Rugby League Chief Executive Maurice Lindsay, writes GEORGE DOWSON.

And how appropriate that was because Lindsay was chairman of Wigan when their sensational run began back in 1987.

He said: "I saw the first of Wigan's run of 43 Cup tie wins and I feel privileged to have been here for the last.

"It was sad because it was like seeing a great champion go down. Wigan have been sensational over the past decade and deserve all the respect from everybody in the game for what they have achieved and for the profile they have given to the game of Rugby League. But Salford deserve all the words of praise that are being heaped upon them.

"I have watched them several times this season and was here to present them with the First Division championship trophy. I have been predicting this could happen. I said it was on the cards.

"This a great day for Rugby League and just think of the tremendous lift Salford have given to the fans of St Helens, Leeds, Bradford and those other clubs still left in the competition." Wigan chairman Jack Robinson said: "This is the end of a great record, one which I think will never be equalled. It took a great side to pull it off and all credit to Salford. They played with more hunger and enthusiasm than we did."

Wigan coach Graeme West was equally generous saying: "Salford deserved their victory and it is going to take a good side to stop them in this mood. They played as well as anybody we have come up against in a long time."

West's assistant, former Great Britain star Joe Lydon added: "It is always a bitter pill to swallow when you lose a record like ours. But it is made a lot easier when you know you have lost to a far better team on the day."

Salford chairman John Wilkinson said: "This is a wonderful day for our club and, hopefully, it will hammer home the message that Salford are fit for Super League and will be worthy members."

And coach Andy Gregory, revelling in the jubilant party mood of a packed Willows Variety Centre said with a huge grin: "I'm not saying we will win the Cup but we've got a better chance than Wigan! It is not beyond us to win it. We have to keep our feet on the ground, wait for the draw and prepare for the quarter-final in the same way as we did for this game."

And Les Bettinson, who joined Salford in 1957 and has served the club as player, coach and director, felt that this victory equalled any in those heady championship-winning days of the seventies.

"This matches anything in all my time at Salford", he said. "It is evocative of that magical time and you can feel that same belief that the players had in themselves in those days."

One of Salford's biggest days in recent history was not when they won a trophy. It was, strangely, the day that they prevented Wigan from winning one! The magnificent Wigan side of the time had won the Rugby League Challenge Cup at Wembley for eight consecutive seasons and created an aura of invincibility in the competition. On 11 February 1996, the renamed Salford Reds defeated them 26-16 in a fifth round tie at The Willows in one of the greatest cup upsets of the decade. This *Manchester Evening News* report perfectly captures the euphoria that was felt by the Salford faithful. Unfortunately for Salford supporters, the fairy tale ended in the next round when Salford lost to the eventual winners, St Helens.

The Salford Reds received the First Division Championship Bowl at the end of the 1996 season. Salford were placed in the First Division (the old Second) after 1994/95 and this was actually the second time they topped the First Division table during the year. In 1995 the Rugby League hierarchy made the momentous decision to switch to a summer schedule from 1996 onwards. To make the adjustment, the 1995/96 season finished in January and was called the Centenary Championship. The new summer season ran from May to September. Salford won both competitions, but only earned promotion to the new Super League after the latter success. The presentation was made on 1 September 1996 after the home match with Hull KR in the Divisional Premiership play-off semi-final. Prop Cliff Eccles – destined to win the Tom Bergin Trophy as man of the match in the following week's Premiership final – with 'devilish' looking supporters Andy Leonard (left) and Tommy Hurst.

Fata Sini, Salford's exciting Samoan winger, captured in a determined run against Hull Kingston Rovers in the semi-final of the Divisional Premiership. Played at The Willows on 1 September 1996, Salford won 36-16 to earn a place in the following weekend's final.

Salford made their second appearance in the Premiership finals at Old Trafford on 8 September 1996. The opposition was Keighley, a much-improved outfit in recent seasons, who had finished second to the Reds in the First Division table. For the Salford loose forward, Sam Panapa, it was the final match in a distinguished career and he crowned it with one of his best ever performances for the Reds. Here we see him on a telling break through the Keighley defence.

The moment of jubilation is captured as the champagne explodes across the Old Trafford pitch following the Reds' victory in the 1996 Divisional Premiership final. Although we can just see the Salford captain Steve Blakely (holding the trophy) and his team through the haze created by the spray, it is a scene that perfectly captures the atmosphere and excitement of the moment.

David Tarry was one of chairman John Wilkinson's earliest recruits in June 1982. Since that time he has been instrumental in taking the club to new heights, both commercially and professionally. Tarry had established a reputation as a successful promotions manager during four years with Oldham Rugby League Club, followed by a year at Bramley, before he joined Salford. Initially, he took on the key role of commercial manager and then, in 1992, his experience and expertise was further recognised when he was given a wider brief in the new post of chief executive. This appointment, in retrospect, can be seen as being ahead of its time, as it is now a dictate of Super League that each member club employs a full-time chief executive.

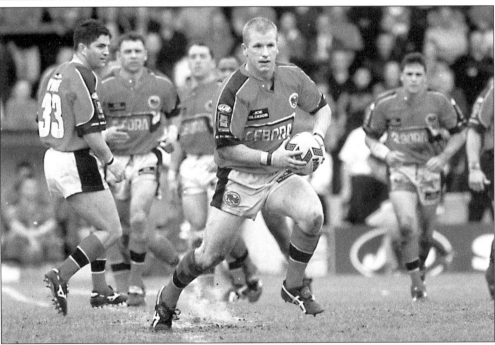

Martin Crompton brings the ball away in a home Super League match against the Castleford Tigers on 31 May 1998. Amongst the sea of Salford Reds players at the back is Australian scrum-half Josh White (33). As Crompton and White were both specialist scrum-halves, Crompton operated for much of the season from the loose-forward berth, although in this match it was White who played out of position at stand-off. The Reds lost this match 18-8 during a disappointing second season in Super League, finishing eleventh of the twelve teams.

Salford received a home draw to Sheffield Eagles in the Rugby League Challenge Cup at the start of the 1999 season on 13 February. Sheffield had defeated Salford in the previous season's semi-final, on the way to a shock victory over Wigan at Wembley. This time the Reds got their revenge with a 16-6 win. In this picture, Salford's classy stand-off Steve Blakeley, on a typical break, looks to set up another attacking move. Blakeley, signed from Wigan in November 1992, is one of the most prolific goal kickers in the game.

More action from the 1999 Challenge Cup win over the Sheffield Eagles as the Salford Reds Cumbrian hero, Gary Broadbent, brings the ball away from his line. The dependable and brave full-back had joined Salford from Widnes in April 1997.

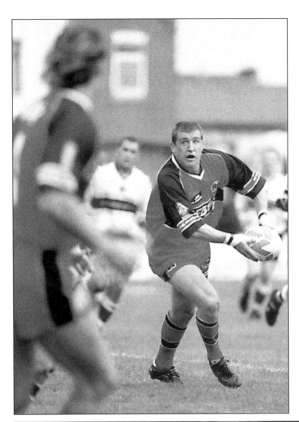

The Salford Reds take on Wakefield Trinity Wildcats in a home Super League fixture on 13 June 1999 as Darren Brown feeds the ball to fellow Australian Paul Carrige (in foreground). Salford won this match 28-14.

Further action from the Salford versus Wakefield Super League clash in 1999 as Paul Highton registers the Reds' second try. It was a season of turmoil for Salford which saw them finish twelfth of the fourteen clubs.

Flying wingman Martin Offiah was a major coup for the Salford City Reds when he signed on the dotted line in November 1999. He had scored more tries than any English player in the game's history and his glittering career includes two Lance Todd Trophy awards as the outstanding player in Rugby League's Wembley showpiece. His capture was seen as a key element in new Aussie coach John Harvey's rebuilding programme for the Super League 2000 campaign.

Simon Svabic in action for Salford City Reds against Warrington Wolves at The Willows on 12 March 2000. The occasion was the televised Rugby League Challenge Cup sixth round tie, which Salford narrowly lost 22-20 in injury time, to miss out on a semi-final place. Svabic, closely watched by skipper Darren Brown (on the left) and Malcolm Alker (right) represents the emerging breed of young stars at Salford.

The new image of the Salford City Reds, complete with Red Devil logo, incorporates the community feeling engendered by the 'Pride of the City' slogan. Adding 'City' to the club name during 1999 was an inspired move and helped raise the profile of a region that is often, incorrectly thought of as a district of Manchester. The new title was officially launched in the televised home match with Gateshead Thunder on 18 July.

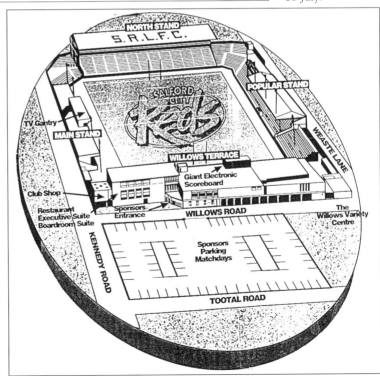

An up-to-date plan of The Willows stadium, the home of the Salford Rugby League Club for almost a century.